New Jersey Firsts

The Famous, Infamous, and Quirky
of the Garden State

Harry Armstrong
and
Tom Wilk

Camino Books, Inc.
Philadelphia

Manufactured in the United States of America

2 3 4 5 01

Library of Congress Cataloging-in-Publication Data

Armstrong, Harry, 1958-
    New Jersey firsts : the famous, infamous, and quirky of the Garden
  State / Harry Armstrong and Tom Wilk.
        p.   cm.
    Includes bibliographical references.
    ISBN 0-940159-45-7 (alk. paper)
     1. New Jersey—History—Miscellanea.   I. Wilk, Tom.   II. Title.
  F134.6.A76   1999
  974.9—dc21   98-55151

Many of the designations used by manufacturers and sellers to distinguish their products are claimed as trademarks. Where those designations appear in this book, and Camino Books, Inc., was aware of a trademark claim, the designations have been printed in caps or initial caps.

Cover and interior design: Jerilyn Bockorick

This book is available at a special discount on bulk purchases for promotional, business, and educational use.

For information write:
Camino Books, Inc.
P.O. Box 59026
Philadelphia, PA 19102

www.caminobooks.com

To Susan and my sons,
Ryan, Eric, and Alex.—H. A.

To my mother, my wife, Elizabeth,
and my daughters, Maria and Julia.—T. W.

CONTENTS

ACKNOWLEDGMENTS

All books are a collaborative effort. The authors thank the following for their contributions to this book: *Atlantic City Magazine*; Burlington County Historical Society; John Campbell; Campbell Soup Co.; William Gallagher; Garden State Park; Bob and Helen Guastavino; Vicki Gold Levi and the Atlantic City Historical Museum; the *Golden Times* newspaper; Skip Hidlay and the photo archives of the *Courier-Post* newspaper; Bill Himmelman of Sports Nostalgia Research; Edith Hoelle and the Gloucester County Historical Society Library; the Horse Racing Hall of Fame in Saratoga, New York; Dr. Harvey Kornberg of Rider University; Lucent Technologies; the Marbles Hall of Fame in Wildwood; Barbara V. Michalsky; the Museum of American Glass at Wheaton Village; the National Collegiate Athletic Association; the New Jersey Department of Education; the New Jersey Department of Transportation; the New Jersey Inventors Hall of Fame; *New Jersey Monthly* magazine; the New Jersey State Museum, Trenton; H. V. Pat Reilly and the New Jersey State Aviation Hall of Fame and Museum in Teterboro; the Seabrook Educational and Cultural Center in Upper Deerfield; Ben Vaughn and Rhino Records; and Carol Hupping for Camino Books.

Harry Armstrong
Tom Wilk

New Jersey Firsts is about success and winning. It's about the creativity, hard work, and risk-taking that have led to monumental (and sometimes mundane, but nonetheless intriguing) achievements within our state.

New Jersey has played a dramatic role in the evolution of our country in so many respects—from agriculture to medicine, technology to recreation. Legends like Thomas Edison and the great minds at Bell Labs made New Jersey a worldwide leader in enterprise and innovation; they played a big part in putting the "high" in high technology. And where would commerce be today without the bar code system...cooks without Teflon-coated frying pans, canned soup, and frozen vegetables...golfers without tees? And where would we all be without the adhesive bandage, the succulent blueberry, air conditioning, and the touch-tone telephone? All are New Jersey firsts.

The state is essentially defined by its accomplishments. Our agricultural foundation still thrives; the "Garden State" established national prominence through such innovative companies as Campbell Soup and Seabrook Farms. Our beaches, boardwalks, and shore resorts—Cape May and Atlantic City, to name but two—to this day serve as the heart of much of the region's tourism. The incredible legacy of the state's pharmaceutical industry has aided millions of people around the world and has set corporate standards for companies well beyond the state's borders.

New Jersey certainly has taken its shots; stand-up comedians have been making sure of that for years. (No, New Jersey is *not* responsible for the first mosquito the size of a sparrow.) But we can take a punch—and we can even take a poke at ourselves, as you'll see when you read the story about a design guaranteed to give automobile drivers and passengers sweaty palms: the notorious traffic circle.

As lifelong residents of New Jersey, we were familiar with some of our home state's claims before we started on this book. But we had no idea just how rich in firsts this part of the country is. New Jersey ranks 46th in size among the 50 states, but it is second to none in its creativity. Our research turned up far more firsts than the pages of this book could hold. And the many photos and wonderful little stories we discovered took us back in time and brought to life so many of the fascinating people, places, things, and events that make this small state so very colorful.

Now it's your time to find out about New Jersey's claims to fame. Read the book, look at the pictures, and you, too, will then know who pitched the first perfect game in Little League World Series history, how salt water taffy came to be, where the first Indian reservation was located, how a New Jersey man gave us standardized time, who built the Navy's first submarine...and much more.

Our Forefathers' Firsts

FIRST LOG HOUSES IN NORTH AMERICA

Harry and Doris Rink are literally living in the past. The Gibbstown, Gloucester County, residents own the C. A. Nothnagle Log House, the last remaining log home built by Swedish settlers between 1638 and 1643. The Gloucester County homes were among the first log cabins built in North America, making the Nothnagle Cabin the oldest log cabin still standing on the continent.

The cabin is a silent witness to life in the earliest days of colonial America, more than 125 years before the Declaration of Independence was signed. The cabin has been placed on the National Register of

The C. A. Nothnagle Log Cabin in the Gibbstown section of Greenwich is the oldest in the country. The interior includes a spinning wheel and the original fireplace. *Courtesy of the* Courier-Post

Historic Sites and has been preserved to an extent that it could still be recognized by the original owners.

"We've done a lot of work on the house, but we'll never be done," said Harry Rink, who has owned the cabin since 1969. The Rinks live in additions that were built onto the original cabin in the 18th and 19th centuries. No exact date has been determined for the cabin's construction, but it is known that settlers from Sweden arrived in Delaware in 1638 and traveled up the Delaware River to present-day Greenwich. At the time, much of the area around the cabin was wetlands and the cabin's site was chosen because it was a spot on dry land near the Delaware River.

Small Is Beautiful

The cabin is 16 feet by 22 feet and was constructed without nails. The corners are dovetailed to ensure a tight fit in order to keep out winter's snow and cold. There are no bedrooms in the cabin; bedrolls were laid out in the evening and put away during the day to create more space. The cabin originally had an earthen floor, but pine boards made of lob lolly pine, a tree that no longer grows in South Jersey, were added in 1730.

The cabin also features a brick fireplace in the corner, a trademark of Swedish log homes. The fireplace's location offers maximum warmth to occupants, an important feature needed to combat harsh winters. It is believed that the bricks used to build the fireplace served as ballast on board the ships that brought the Swedes to America.

After the Rinks purchased the cabin, the floor boards were removed and a treasure trove of artifacts was found, including wood-carved cigar holders, glass bottles, and clay marbles. These articles and many others are on display in the house.

☞ To Visit: C. A. Nothnagle Log House

As caretakers of the historical site, Harry and Doris Rink have opened the cabin doors to visitors since 1973 "by chance or by appointment." Periodic open houses are held throughout the year. School groups often visit the cabin, which has received visitors from as far away as Japan, Australia, England, and India.

C. A. Nothnagle Log House
406 Swedesboro Road
Gibbstown, NJ 08027
609-423-0916
Hours: Irregular; call before visiting.

RATIFICATION OF THE BILL OF RIGHTS

When the U.S. Constitution took effect on March 4, 1789, replacing the Articles of Confederation as a framework for the new government, political leaders in some states felt their job was only half done. The new document offered no guarantees of individual freedoms or liberties that the American Revolution had been fought over. It was not a minor issue among the states. Rhode Island, for example, withheld its approval of the Constitution until these rights were spelled out. The Bill of Rights, which was introduced at the first session of Congress on September 25, 1789, as amendments to the Constitution, was intended to correct these oversights, for it clearly enumerated the freedoms enjoyed by the new American citizens.

Major Support in New Jersey

New Jersey's legislature and Governor William Livingston were at the forefront in supporting the Bill of Rights. New Jersey became the first state to ratify the Bill of Rights in November 1789—less than two months after its introduction in Congress.

There was no doubt where the legislators stood when they met in Perth Amboy, Middlesex County. The Bill of Rights was approved unanimously by the Assembly and Legislative Council, the forerunner of the state Senate, on November 19 and 20, respectively. The guarantees of freedom of speech, freedom of the press, freedom of religion, and freedom to assemble and petition the government for redress of grievances would be the foundation of American democracy. Other rights guaranteed in the first 10 constitutional amendments include the right to be free of unreasonable searches and seizures, the right to a speedy and public trial, and the right to a trial by jury in a civil case.

Virginia became the ninth state to ratify the Bill of Rights on December 15, 1791, making the 10 amendments part of the Constitution. It took a little more than two years for the first 10 amendments to the Constitution to be ratified. It would take 139 years for the next 10 amendments to be ratified.

BRITISH PARLIAMENT'S EARLIER ACTIONS

One hundred years before the introduction of the Bill of Rights in the United States, the British Parliament passed its own Bill of Rights in 1689, spelling out the rights of the people and the rights of Parliament.

PURCHASE OF LAND BY THE U.S. GOVERNMENT

The ink was barely dry on the Declaration of Independence when the fledgling government of the United States made its first purchase of land in early July 1776. Ninety-six acres in the Billingsport section of Paulsboro, Gloucester County, were purchased for £600 in Pennsylvania currency from Margaret M. Paul, widow of John Paul, and Benjamin Weathersby, her son by a previous marriage. The land was part of a 100-acre parcel the family owned. The ground was purchased on July 4, 1776, and was deeded to the Thirteen United Colonies a day later, on July 5. Michael Hilegas, the first treasurer of the United States, and George Clymer, a signer of the Declaration of Independence from Pennsylvania, represented the new government and the Continental Congress in the transaction.

The parcel of land was important for military reasons because of its location along the Delaware River and its proximity to Philadelphia. It would be a prime spot for a fort. On July 15, an additional £50 was paid for the remaining four acres of land and a house on it that would be used as a tavern.

General Washington's Approval

Members of the Continental Army from New Jersey, Pennsylvania, Virginia, and South Carolina began to build military fortifications that would become Fort Billings. At one point, more than 1,000 soldiers and workmen were employed during its construction. General George Washington was an ardent advocate of the fort, urging its completion in the summer of 1777. Washington inspected the fort on August 1 of that year.

Robert Smith, a Revolutionary War patriot, designed underwater barricades, a series of iron-tipped wooden spikes that were sunk in the Delaware River near Fort Billings. The barricades were weighted down with large stones and placed in the river so that the logs were four feet below the water's surface and made it difficult for enemy ships to travel along the river.

The defensive strategy initially prevented the British military from coming up the Delaware and getting in position to attack Philadelphia. Instead, British forces were diverted and traveled up the Chesapeake Bay. As a result, Washington reassigned many of his troops along the Delaware River to defend against the British from the south. After the Battle of Brandywine, the British were able to capture Fort Billings because there were so few soldiers to defend it. The British forces came over from Pennsylvania and were able to remove some of the underwater barricades to create safe passage for their boats. There were a little more than 100 men inside the fort at the time of its capture.

Fort Billings also was used by the military during the War of 1812. General Ebenezer Elmer directed the rehabilitation of the fort and established it as a training center. In 1814, more than 2,000 soldiers from the fort were dispatched to New York City to bolster defenses there. In 1815, the fort was mustered out of service and never again would be used by the military.

New Jersey was a fitting place for the first land purchase by the United States government. The state would be known as the "Cockpit of the Revolution" for the important Revolutionary War battles fought on its soil. They included the Battle of Trenton (1776), the Battle of Princeton (1777), and the Battle of Morristown (1778).

CAPITAL CITIES IN NEW JERSEY

Two New Jersey cities, Trenton and Princeton, briefly served as the capital of the United States between the end of the Revolutionary War and the adoption of the Constitution.

A SMALL PRICE TO PAY

The purchase of Fort Billings would pale next to the Louisiana Purchase. In 1803, the federal government paid less than three cents an acre for 828,000 square miles of land in the western half of the Mississippi River Basin from French emperor Napoleon Bonaparte. Total price for the Louisiana Purchase, including interest, came to $27,267,622.

"There are no second acts in American lives," observed novelist and former Princeton University student F. Scott Fitzgerald.

You couldn't prove it by Grover Cleveland, who experienced the highest highs and lowest lows of American politics in an eight-year span. The New Jersey native became the first man to serve two non-consecutive terms as president, winning election in 1884 and then again in 1892. Those victories were sandwiched around a defeat to Benjamin Harrison in 1888.

Born in Caldwell, Essex County, on March 18, 1837, Cleveland moved to Buffalo, New York, where he practiced law and became active in Democratic politics. He became mayor of Buffalo in 1881 and governor of New York in 1883. The Democratic Party, which had not won a presiden-

President Grover Cleveland appeared on the 22-cent postage stamp issued as part of the Presidential Series in 1938. Cleveland was the first man to serve two non-consecutive terms as president.
Courtesy of Tom Wilk

tial election since 1856, nominated Cleveland, a rising star in the party, to run for president in 1884, based on his success as a reformer.

Morality Issues, Even Then

Cleveland defeated James G. Blaine, his Republican opponent, in a hotly contested campaign. Cleveland had admitted fathering a child out of wedlock and the Republicans tried to capitalize on the morality issue with the slogan "Ma, ma, where's my pa?" The Democrats came up with their rejoinder: "Gone to the White House, ha, ha, ha."

In his first term, Cleveland continued his reforms. He ordered that more than 12,000 federal jobs be protected under a new civil service law and not be subjected to the whims of political patronage. Cleveland's opposition to a high protective tariff on the import of foreign goods was the key issue of his first term, and it dominated his campaign against Harrison in 1888.

A TURNPIKE TRIBUTE

Grover Cleveland achieved an immortality of sorts by having a rest stop named for him on the New Jersey Turnpike. It is located at milepost 92.9 north in Woodbridge Township, Middlesex County.

Cleveland won the popular vote but lost to Harrison in the electoral college. Cleveland returned to the practice of law in New York City but retained an interest in politics. In 1892, he ran against Harrison and James Weaver, the candidate of the newly formed Populist Party. He won a majority of electoral votes and had a plurality in the popular vote. Cleveland's second term was marked by an economic depression in 1893, and he fell out of favor with his party. The Republicans regained the White House with the election of William McKinley in 1896.

Cleveland returned to New Jersey after completing his second term in March 1897. He settled in Princeton and became a lecturer and trustee at Princeton University. He also did legal work for insurance companies. In his later years, he was warmly remembered for the integrity he had shown in office. He died in Princeton on June 24, 1908, at the age of 71. His final words summed up his life well: "I have tried so hard to do right."

NEW JERSEY BOOSTS DEMOCRATIC PARTY

The Democratic Party won only four presidential elections between 1860 and 1928. All four triumphs involved men with ties to New Jersey. Besides Grover Cleveland's two victories, Woodrow Wilson, who served as governor of New Jersey, won presidential elections in 1912 and 1916.

E PLURIBUS UNUM

E pluribus unum, the Latin phrase meaning "out of many, one," is a familiar motto on the penny, nickel, dime, and quarter. However, it appeared on a coin for the first time on "Horse Head Coppers," which were produced in New Jersey during the 1780s.

An act of the New Jersey legislature in 1786 authorized the production of three million coins within a two-year period. Each coin contained 150 grains of pure copper, and the value of each copper was set at $\frac{1}{15}$ of a shilling. Members of the Supreme Court determined the inscriptions and marks on each.

Walter Mould, Albion Cox, and Thomas Goadily were awarded the contract to manufacture the coins. In return, each had to give the state treasury one-tenth of the coins produced at his mint every three months. The three mints were located in Morristown, Elizabethtown, and Rahway.

Some scholars have theorized that the use of *e pluribus unum* could have been included on coins to promote the idea of a federal government. Two employees who worked at the Rahway mint later were employed at the federal mint. The 13 states were loosely affiliated under the Articles of Confederation, which would be replaced by the U.S. Constitution. The Constitution was signed in September 1787 and took effect when the state of New York became the ninth state to ratify it, in 1788.

States were allowed to produce their own coins under the Articles of Confederation, but later that power was restricted to the federal government under the U.S. Constitution.

LUCKY THIRTEEN

In a numerical coincidence, *e pluribus unum* has 13 letters, the same as the number of original states.

MOST COMPLETE DINOSAUR SKELETON

New Jersey's role in the discovery of dinosaurs traces back to Haddonfield, Camden County, where in 1858, William Parker Foulke dug up what was then the most complete dinosaur skeleton ever found. Indeed, the *Hadrosaurus foulkii*, as Foulke's discovery was to become known, was the world's first dinosaur skeleton to be mounted and publicly displayed.

As it turns out, though, one of the country's founding fathers, Benjamin Franklin, was presented in 1787 with a heavy, dark bone excavated from Woodbury, Gloucester County. Franklin, then serving as president of the American Philosophical Society, which was meeting in Philadelphia, was informed by prominent Philadelphia physician Caspar Wistar that the

This plaque in Haddonfield commemorates the unearthing of a nearly complete dinosaur skeleton by William Parker Foulke. *Courtesy of the* Courier-Post

HADROSAURUS FOULKII

IN A MARL PIT ON THE JOHN E. HOPKINS FARM IN OCTOBER 1858, THE WORLD'S FIRST NEARLY COMPLETE DINOSAUR SKELETON WAS UNEARTHED BY WILLIAM PARKER FOULKE. THE FIND WAS ADJACENT TO THIS POINT. THIS WAS ALSO THE FIRST DINOSAUR SKELETON TO EVER BE MOUNTED. THE BONES REPRESENTED A 25 FOOT, 7-8 TON, HERBIVOROUS HADROSAURUS (REPTILE). ITS HEIGHT PROBABLY RANGED FROM 6-10 FEET AT THE HIPS. SOME 55 OF AN ESTIMATED 80 BONES WERE DISCOVERED. THIS CREATURE LIVED 70-80 MILLION YEARS AGO DURING THE CRETACEOUS PERIOD AT THE END OF THE DINOSAUR AGE.

THIS SITE WAS DEVELOPED IN 1984 AS AN EAGLE SCOUT PROJECT BY CHRISTOPHER BREES, TROOP 65. MAJOR PROJECT FUNDING BY THE ACADEMY OF NATURAL SCIENCES, PHILADELPHIA, PA.

bone might be a thigh bone from a large man. Ultimately, however, the bone found its way to the Academy of Natural Sciences in Philadelphia where work by Dr. Donald Baird, formerly of Princeton University, led to the conclusion that the bone was the left metatarsal (foot) bone of a duck-billed dinosaur.

Franklin and Wistar can be forgiven for their error in not properly identifying the Woodbury bone. The term "dinosaur" was not even coined until 1842, when it was first used by British comparative anatomist Richard Owen, who worked only with isolated bones and teeth discovered in England in the early 1820s.

Likewise, American dinosaur discoveries were isolated and fragmented until the monumental 1858 excavation of *Hadrosaurus foulkii* from a pit in

Haddonfield, a discovery that effectively earned New Jersey the title of birthplace of North American vertebrate paleontology. Foulke, a member of the Academy of Natural Sciences, was vacationing in Haddonfield when he heard tales of vertebrae bone discoveries that had taken place 20 years earlier from John Hopkins, the proprietor of a local farm. As local legend has it, Hopkins had allowed visitors to carry away those bones for use as door stops and window jams. It was Hopkins' news that motivated Foulke to dig around in Hopkins' marl pit. (Marl is a kind of dark clay that contains fossil seashells and was commonly mined for use as a fertilizer.)

NEW JERSEY'S OWN JURASSIC PARK

William Parker Foulke's 1858 discovery, *Hadrosaurus foulkii*, was designated New Jersey's "state dinosaur" in 1991, and the site of the discovery and excavation along what is now Maple Avenue in Haddonfield was designated a National Historic Landmark in 1995.

Using a team of marl miners, Foulke led the excavation of a series of bones that experts carefully measured, catalogued, and transported to a nearby house. When the digging finally stopped in December 1858, Foulke had discovered the most complete dinosaur skeleton ever, totaling 49 bones and teeth. Casts were made from the bones and missing parts (including the skull, which was never found) were fashioned. In 1868, the Academy of Natural Sciences was presented with the first mounted skeleton of a dinosaur.

INDIAN RESERVATION

For every action there is an equal and opposite reaction. That observation by Sir Isaac Newton turned out to be true when applied to the American Indians living in New Jersey after Europeans began to settle in the state.

Indians, known today as Native Americans, had lived in the region that would become known as New Jersey for at least 60 centuries before settlers from Sweden, the Netherlands, and England began arriving in the 1600s. As the Europeans gained a foothold in New Jersey, problems with infectious diseases (such as smallpox), alcohol, emigration, and poor relations with European settlers contributed to the thinning of the Indian population. The Lenni-Lenape Indian tribe was nearly wiped out by the 1750s.

That turn of events led New Jersey to create the first Indian reservation in the United States in 1758, nearly two decades before the Declaration of Independence was signed. The site was known as Brotherton, located in what is now Shamong and Tabernacle, Burlington County. The reservation consisted of about 3,200 acres, or five square miles of land.

The state took the necessary steps to set up the reservation after a delegation of Indians petitioned the colonial legislature for use of the area in August 1758. The reservation came with a steep price: The remaining Indian tribes relinquished all their claims to New Jersey land for £1,000 in October 1758.

The Indians began moving to Brotherton in 1759, but they were unable to prosper on their new land. A one-room schoolhouse, a church, and a sawmill were built, but the commercial venture failed. The Indians lived on the land until 1801, when they moved to New York after obtaining the permission of the state legislature there. The reservation's land was divided and sold. That was the end of the reservation experiment in New Jersey—but the concept of a reservation for Indians would be revived in other parts of the country in the next century.

Planes, Trains, and Automobiles, Etc.

SHIP-TO-SHORE TELEPHONE CONVERSATION

If you're bemused at the often inappropriate appearance of cellular telephones—no longer are we unreachable at the mall, restaurants, sporting events, or even on airplanes—then blame it on William Rankin and Sir Thomas Lipton. It was those two gentlemen who on December 8, 1929, gave an indication of what would become the ultimately overwhelming reach of the telephone.

Rankin sat in a hotel in Atlantic City and conversed with Lipton as he swayed aboard an ocean liner sailing in the Atlantic during what was the first commercial ship-to-shore telephone call. This operator-assisted phone call took place more than 30 years before the retail introduction of the touch-tone telephone and the initial orbit of Telstar, the first international communications satellite—and 22 years before area codes even existed.

FLIGHT IN THE UNITED STATES

Jean-Pierre Blanchard was confident as he strode across Walnut Street in Philadelphia on the cool, wintry morning of January 9, 1793. Before him stood his aircraft: a green and yellow silk balloon decorated in spangled silver and with a blue basket. The balloon's colorful appearance ensured that it would be easily visible to the naked eye. Blanchard hoped to set an aviation milestone by successfully completing the first balloon flight in the history of the United States.

Deptford publicizes its connection with the first flight in the United States by including balloons on its street and road signs.
Photo by Tom Wilk

Blanchard had a track record of success. He began his ballooning career in 1784 and made the first balloon flight in Great Britain that same year. On January 7, 1785, he and John Jeffries, a physician from the United States, made the first balloon crossing of the English Channel. The trip was not an easy one. The two men had to throw everything they had with them overboard to keep the balloon airborne so that it would make it to the French coast near Calais.

Tickets for Sale

At 39 years old, the Frenchman Blanchard came to Philadelphia in December 1792 to promote his balloon flight. He sold tickets at five dollars—a considerably high price for the late 18th century—to watch the liftoff of his balloon from the courtyard of the prison at Sixth and Walnut Streets in the city.

Jean-Pierre Blanchard made the first balloon flight from Philadelphia to Deptford, New Jersey, on January 9, 1793.
Courtesy of Library of Congress collection

There was a festive atmosphere in Philadelphia on the morning of the flight. The sound of cannons reverberated in the streets in the hours before Blanchard began his trip. President George Washington, living in Philadelphia, then the U.S. capital, personally wished him well and gave him a letter ordering all Americans to pose "no hindrance or molestation to the balloonist wherever he should land."

Amid much fanfare and the accompaniment of a band, Blanchard began his historic trip at 10:09 A.M., his balloon traveling southeast across the Delaware River toward New Jersey. It would land 45 minutes later in a farmer's field in Deptford Township, Gloucester County, about 15 miles from his starting point. Blanchard spoke no English and the farmer spoke no French, but Washington's letter ensured the balloonist's safety after Blanchard met a resident who could read English.

After getting over the shock of Blanchard's arrival by balloon, Deptford residents treated the Frenchman as a hero, thanks in part to his sharing the wine that was aboard his gondola. He was treated to dinner at a nearby tavern and returned to Philadelphia by carriage and ferry at seven that evening.

Aviation Pioneer

Blanchard had written the first chapter in the history of American aviation that would see unprecedented achievements in the next two centuries. And he was a fitting choice to make the first flight in the United States: he was born on July 4, 1753, 23 years to the day before the Declaration of Independence was signed.

After that landing in Deptford, Blanchard would continue ballooning for another 15 years until he suffered a heart attack during a flight over Paris in 1808. He died a year later of heart failure.

A PLACE IN SPACE

New Jersey also played a role in the first manned landing on the moon, on July 20, 1969. Astronaut Edwin "Buzz" Aldrin, the second man to walk on the moon, came from Montclair, Essex County. In an interesting twist, his mother's maiden name was Moon.

STEAM FERRY AND STEAM LOCOMOTIVE

When Colonel John Stevens designed, built, and tested the country's first steam locomotive, it by no means immediately blazed new trails in the transportation of people or goods. After all, just who wanted to travel by rail in short circles on Stevens' estate in Hoboken, Hudson County? But Stevens' first steam locomotive, running on that circular track in 1826, ultimately led him and his family to the forefront of what would be incredible advances in the country's railroads.

John Stevens studied law and served as treasurer of New Jersey from 1776 to 1777. In 1784, he purchased a large tract of land and essentially laid out the town of Hoboken around his estate in 1804. His first forays into steam power resulted in the steamboat *Little Juliana*, which sailed from Hoboken across the Hudson River to New York City in 1804, and the paddle-wheel steamboat *Phoenix*, which made the first steam-powered ocean voyage when it sailed from New York City to Philadelphia in 1809. Stevens later ran the country's first successful steam ferry, operating between Hoboken and New York City, beginning in 1811.

Turning to Dry Land

Having conquered the seas, Stevens then turned his attention to the shores. He rationalized that if a steam ferry could economically haul people and freight, then a steam-operated railroad could do the same. Stevens obtained the first railroad charter in the United States on February 6, 1815. A little more than a decade later, he had his steam "wagon" operating on the circular track in Hoboken.

Stevens' second son, Robert Livingston Stevens, was granted the state's first commercial railroad charter for the Camden and Amboy Railroad and Transportation Company (C&A RR) in 1830. Robert Stevens carved out his own place in railroad breakthroughs by designing the first T-shaped rail, the "hook-headed" spike used to fasten rails, and the "iron tongue" used to join rails.

Innovations in Rail Safety

In 1863, Ashbel Welch, an employee of the C&A RR, developed the "all clear ahead" signal system, which combined the use of the telegraph and a manually operated sign. Two decades later, the first fully automatic "all clear ahead" signal was used in Phillipsburg, Warren County. It was Welch who also designed the first interlocking switch system. This system sets all the switches at a junction in order to decrease the chances of a train derailment. It was first used on the Pennsylvania Railroad in East Newark, Hudson County, in 1875.

The Stevens Institute of Technology

Edwin Augustus Stevens, the sixth son of John Stevens, played a significant role in the family's steam success, primarily by managing the family's finances. He did, however, invent a plow and a wagon for hauling garbage (1823) and personally financed, built, and demonstrated the feasibility of an ironclad warship (1844). He served as treasurer (1830) and president (1854) of the C&A RR, and it was he who bequeathed the money and land to found the Hoboken-based Stevens Institute of Technology, a four-year college with undergraduate and graduate programs in technology.

PATERSON—LEADER IN LOCOMOTIVES

While Hoboken served as the birthplace of the Stevens family's steam inventions, it was the city of Paterson, Passaic County, that became the nation's preeminent producer of steam locomotives. The factory of Rogers, Ketchem & Grosvenor built the first steam locomotive in 1837, and by 1850 the plant was building more than 100 locomotives per year. Other Paterson locomotive companies were Swinburne, Smith & Company and Danforthe, Cooke & Company. The plants of these three companies covered almost 15 acres of the city of Paterson and produced more than 5,800 locomotives by 1881.

☞ *To Visit: Paterson Museum*

The museum features exhibits chronicling the history of steam locomotives in New Jersey.

Paterson Museum
2 Market Street
Paterson, NJ 07501
973-881-3874
Hours: Tuesday-Friday, 10 A.M.-4 P.M.; Saturday-Sunday, 12:30-4:30 P.M.
Admission charged.

USE OF THE WORD *AIRPORT*

The word *airport* has been a part of the English language for more than 75 years, but few people know that the word originated in South Jersey.

Bader Field in Atlantic City, Atlantic County, located less than half a mile from the Boardwalk, was not the first place in the United States where airplanes could take off and land. But it was the first facility to be called an "airport."

The question of who came up with the term in 1919 has never been resolved. In his book *From the Balloon to the Moon*, a history of aviation in New Jersey, author H. V. Pat Reilly offers up two possible answers. Atlantic City businessman Henry Woodhouse, one of the guiding forces behind Bader Field, noted Atlantic City was a prime location for a *sea*port, so why not an *air*port? Others credit William Dill, then the editor of the *Atlantic City Press*, with coining the term. Whoever was responsible, that person came up with a word that is now in use around the world.

AROUND THE WORLD WITHOUT NAVIGATIONAL INSTRUMENTS

Like the child who isn't happy just riding his two-wheeler and must take the feat to another level—"Look Mom, no hands!"—Marvin Creamer took sailing around the world to the next plateau—"Look Mom, no modern navigational instruments!"

Creamer, a former Glassboro, Gloucester County, resident and geography professor at Glassboro State College (now Rowan University), became the first man to pilot a sailboat around the world without the aid of modern navigational equipment when he set sail on the Delaware River from National Park, Gloucester County, on December 15, 1982, and returned safely to a hero's welcome at Red Bank Battlefield in National Park some 17 months later on May 21, 1984.

The journey was completed in four stages in the 35-foot steel yacht *Globe Star*. Creamer (age 68 when the trip was completed) and his crew included nine different persons throughout the journey, but there were never more than three persons aboard at one time. They sailed first from New Jersey across the Atlantic Ocean to Cape Town, South Africa. Then they crossed the Indian Ocean to Hobart, Tasmania, off the southern tip of Australia. The third leg of the journey took them across the Pacific Ocean and around Cape Horn to the Falkland Islands. Finally, Creamer and his crew sailed the Atlantic home to New Jersey. During the 17-month journey, the yacht was at sea for as long as three months at a time and traveled approximately 30,000 miles.

Marvin Creamer sailed around the world in the *Globe Star*, a 35-foot yacht.
Courtesy of the Courier-Post

Simply sailing around the world in a 35-foot yacht is a feat in and of itself. But completing this journey without so much as a compass or sextant puts the accomplishment in a league of its own. Professor Creamer circumnavigated the globe primarily by reading the positions of the stars to fix his location—the same way sailors did before modern navigational conveniences.

The trip "reminded us that navigation is as much an art as a science," said Lee Houchins, who directed computerized tracking of the *Globe Star* for the Smithsonian Institution. It was noted that 10th-century Vikings had more equipment to guide them on the seas than Creamer, who also used the winds, the currents, and speed estimates based on passing bubbles to plot his course.

WORLD WAR II DOGFIGHT VICTORY

The aerial dogfights of World War II are legendary today, well documented in movies, television, books, and VFW halls around the country. But for Captain Frank A. Hill, a former high school athlete from Hillsdale, Bergen County, flying the skies of Europe in his Spitfire V fighter plane in 1942 was far from glamorous. In August 1942, Hill, then just 23, became the first American pilot to shoot down a German fighter plane, recording America's initial aerial victory in a war where dogfights were scored like sporting events.

According to the Associated Press, Hill shot down a Focke-Wulf 190, Germany's newest and then-fastest fighter plane, for the first kill of World War II—though Hill never saw the enemy plane crash, so he reported it as a "probable." United Press International reported the same result as the AP, calling Hill a "hero of one American formation...jumped by an overwhelming force of Focke-Wulfs." The U.S. formation "was not able to get help from other Allied squadrons, which were driving off German bombers," so Hill's formation had "to wage a lone fight against some of Germany's top pilots," UPI reported.

First Real Combat

Hill is quoted in the book *From the Balloon to the Moon:*

> Just like all these fellows [pilots in his squadron], it was my first real taste of combat. I was leading my flight over Dieppe when several Focke-Wulfs came down from the clouds behind us. We were just turning to meet them when one crossed my sights. I gave him a four-second burst with cannon and machine guns and he acted like he was hit pretty bad. I must have got both the pilot and the engine. He smoked a little and spun down. He came out of the spin near the ground but then fell off again. His pals were still around though so I had no chance to watch him all the way.

The August 31, 1942, issue of *Time* magazine confirms that Hill's dogfight was the first U.S. victory and said his scoring of the fight as a "probable" was merely modesty. Hill's military career flourished; he flew 166 combat missions and recorded seven official "kills." He was ultimately promoted to the rank of U.S. Air Force colonel in 1951 and retired from the military in 1969, running the family real estate business in Denville, Morris County. Captain Frank A. Hill was inducted into the Aviation Hall of Fame of New Jersey in 1992.

☞ *To Visit: Aviation Hall of Fame of New Jersey*

Originally organized as the Teterboro Aviation Hall of Fame in 1973, the Aviation Hall of Fame of New Jersey (the name was changed in 1979 through a bill signed by Governor Brendan Byrne) is itself the first state aviation hall of fame in the country. The Hall of Fame includes a museum housed on the grounds of the Teterboro Airport in Teterboro, Bergen County.

Aviation Hall of Fame of New Jersey
Teterboro Airport
Industrial Avenue
Teterboro, NJ 07608
201-288-6344
Hours: Tuesday-Sunday, 10 A.M.-4 P.M.
Suggested donation is $5 for adults, $3 for seniors and children.

FIRST TRANSCONTINENTAL HIGHWAY

The invention of the automobile forever changed the transportation habits of 20th-century Americans. However, the conditions of the early roads—in some cases, little more than glorified dirt trails—were better suited for the horse and buggy of the 19th century.

The Lincoln Highway, the first transcontinental highway in the United States established with cars in mind, was a pioneering road in the history of American transportation. Covering 3,389 miles from Times Square in New York City to Lincoln Park in San Francisco, the Lincoln Highway passed through 12 states, including about 90 miles in New Jersey. From east to west, it went through New York, New Jersey, Pennsylvania, Ohio, Indiana, Illinois, Iowa, Nebraska, Wyoming, Utah, Nevada, and California.

From Newark to Trenton and Beyond

Motorists leaving New York City took an auto ferry to Jersey City and went through the city streets of Newark and Elizabeth to Princeton and Trenton, then over the Delaware River into Pennsylvania. Other New Jersey towns along the route of the Lincoln Highway include Rahway, Menlo Park, Metuchen, New Brunswick, and Lawrence Township. In New Jersey, portions of the Lincoln Highway followed the old Kings' Highway that ran between Philadelphia and New York in colonial times.

The Lincoln Highway was dedicated in 1913, at a time when automobiles were becoming popular in the United States. By 1910, there were 180,000 cars in the country, and the need for a transcontinental highway was becoming more and more apparent. With personal long-distance transportation increasingly available, Americans got the urge to travel beyond their hometowns and states. Early roads often were unpaved and ungraded, and many flooded out in heavy rain. It was not uncommon for a motorist to have more than 100 flat tires when traveling from coast to coast in the early years of the 20th century. And motorists couldn't count on finding service stations along the way; they were few and far between. Motorists had to serve as their own mechanics.

The Lincoln Highway connected the country from the Atlantic to the Pacific, from New York to California. While the road would later be made obsolete by the interstate highway system, the Lincoln Highway represented one more taming of the American frontier.

OTHER NAMES WERE CONSIDERED

The Lincoln Highway was named for Abraham Lincoln, the 16th president of the United States. The name was chosen over several other contenders, including the Coast-to-Coast Rock Highway, the Ocean-to-Ocean Highway, and the American Road.

TRAFFIC CIRCLE

In the years after World War II, two words had the power to make New Jersey drivers break into a cold sweat: traffic circles. Built to facilitate a smooth flow of traffic where several busy roads meet, circles often had the opposite effect on drivers trying to negotiate the 360-degree nightmare during rush hour, when it looked like all drivers had the right of way.

Traffic approaches the Airport Circle in Pennsauken in 1959. The circle was the first of its kind in the United States. *Courtesy of the* Courier-Post

It seemed like a good idea when the first circle in the United States—the Airport Circle in Pennsauken, Camden County—opened in 1925. However, increases in population and Americans' love affair with the automobile would prove otherwise.

The Airport Circle was built where Admiral Wilson Boulevard and routes 38, 70, and 130 converged. It became associated with Central Airport, which opened in 1929, and became one of the busiest circles in the country. The Airport Circle kept its name even after the airport itself closed in 1956.

Frequent Traffic Jams

With only small numbers of cars on the road in the 1920s, the circle worked—it allowed drivers and vehicles to reach their destinations in a timely fashion. By the early 1940s, though, traffic jams were so frequent an occurrence that some local politicians suggested they might hamper the war effort. The Germans and Japanese were defeated in 1945, but the traffic headaches of the Airport Circle would linger for almost half a century.

Overpasses were added after 1945 to alleviate tie-ups, but the growth of suburbs in South Jersey increased traffic again around the circle. On December 11, 1953, a Friday afternoon two weeks before Christmas, a traffic jam at the circle tied up vehicles for almost three hours. A report in the *Courier-Post* newspaper called it "the granddaddy of all tie-ups in this area."

It was not until the 1990s that the Airport Circle finally would be tamed. Following the elimination of the Racetrack Circle and the Ellisburg Circle in nearby Cherry Hill, the Airport Circle was reconfigured and a system of traffic lights was installed. When work was completed in 1995, it made for easier and safer passage there—and for a lot less perspiration from South Jersey drivers.

PAYING FOR IMPROVEMENTS

New Jersey was the first state in the nation to acknowledge a state's responsibility for road improvements and to provide a way to fund these improvements when it passed the State Aid Act in 1891.

ON THE DECLINE

At its peak in the early 1970s, New Jersey had 67 traffic circles, according to the New Jersey Department of Transportation. That number had fallen to 40 by 1998, and the state continues to eliminate more circles.

TRAFFIC CLOVERLEAF

New Jersey is clearly a leader in traffic control innovations. Four years after the introduction of the first traffic circle, the state unveiled the first cloverleaf intersection, in Woodbridge, Middlesex County, where New Jersey Route 35 and U.S. Route 1 converge.

The cloverleaf is a road plan passing one highway over another and routing turning traffic onto connecting highways that branch only to the right, thus allowing traffic to merge without left-hand turns or direct crossings. From the air, the cloverleaf resembles a four-leaf clover or a pair of figure eights.

Arthur Hill patented the cloverleaf idea in 1916, but he would have to wait more than a decade for it to be put into practice. Work on the cloverleaf, in the Iselin section of Woodbridge, began in 1928 and was completed in 1929 at a cost of $276,000.

The cloverleaf design was a popular one at the start. It was heralded as an intersection without "conflict"—a road engineering term for one car needing to stop for another. By 1960, the cloverleaf began to be used less as the number of vehicles on the road increased. Cloverleafs were criticized for taking up too much land, causing accidents, and slowing down traffic.

THE NATIONAL FLOWER?

Cloverleafs were becoming so common by 1940 that architecture critic Lewis Mumford, with tongue planted firmly in cheek, nominated the concrete cloverleaf as the national flower.

For the Health of It

THE NEW JERSEY KNEE

Recipients of artificial knees find it easier to move around now, thanks to the New Jersey Low Contact Stress Total Knee Replacement System. Michael Pappas of Caldwell and Frederick Buechel of South Orange, both in Essex County, designed the system known as the New Jersey Knee in 1974. Pappas was a biomechanics instructor at the University of Medicine and Dentistry in Newark when he asked Buechel, an orthopedic surgeon, to help him build a better knee implant.

An Improvement over Others

The New Jersey Knee was the first to feature multiple parts and a mobile bearing design to allow for more flexible movement plus less wear under pressure. It was an improvement over previous prosthetics. Since its invention, nearly one million people around the world have increased their mobility.

Both Pappas and Buechel have extensive ties to New Jersey. They own Endotec Inc. of South Orange and Bloomfield. Buechel practices with the South Mountain Orthopedic Associates, South Orange, and serves on the clinical faculty of the University of Medicine and Dentistry of New Jersey (UMDNJ) medical school. Pappas, a Newark native, holds bachelor's and master's degrees from the New Jersey Institute of Technology and is an adjunct associate professor of surgery at UMDNJ-Newark.

The collaboration between Michael Pappas and Frederick Buechel goes beyond the New Jersey Knee. They also have developed total replacement systems for the ankle, hip, and shoulder. The two men were inducted into the New Jersey Inventors Hall of Fame in 1998.

MACHINE-MADE SELF-ADHESIVE BANDAGE—THE BAND-AID

The Johnson & Johnson Company was founded by Robert Wood Johnson and his two brothers, James Wood and Edward, in New Brunswick, Middlesex County, in 1886 on the fourth floor of a small building that was once a wallpaper factory. Recognizing the danger associated with wound infection through airborne germs (post-operative mortality rates were as high as 90 percent in some hospitals), the company became the pioneer in ready-made, ready-to-use, sterile surgical dressings, and effectively introduced the first practical application of the concept of antiseptic wound treatment.

The company developed a revolutionary surgical dressing and also designed a soft, absorbent cotton-and-gauze dressing that could be mass-produced and shipped in quantity to hospitals and pharmacies. The company's incredible role in the pharmaceutical industry continues to this day—Johnson & Johnson is now a family of more than 180 companies that market health care products ranging from baby oil to Tylenol, contact lenses to prescription pharmaceuticals, in more than 175 countries.

The Signature Product

To this day, one health care aid remains Johnson & Johnson's signature product—the Band-Aid Brand Adhesive Bandage. The Band-Aid—the term itself a trademark of Johnson & Johnson—made its first appearance on the market in 1921. The bandages were made by hand and were far from an instant success. In that first year, Johnson & Johnson sold just $3,000 worth of Band-Aids. In 1924, however, Johnson & Johnson introduced a new and improved Band-Aid, this one the first-ever machine-made, mass-produced, self-adhesive bandage.

The Band-Aid, a medicine-cabinet must in homes with small, scrape-prone children, offers its own interesting time line. For example, the little red string that helps open the paper Band-Aid package made its first appearance in 1940. In 1956, Johnson & Johnson began marketing the first decorated adhesive bandages and in 1963, Band-Aids traveled in space with the Project Mercury astronauts.

The company's latest Band-Aid innovation was introduced in 1998, when Johnson & Johnson became the first company to market an adhesive bandage that comes pre-coated with an antibiotic ointment. The new product, called the Band-Aid Brand Antibiotic Adhesive Bandage, is far from high-tech—it simply combines treatment (the antibiotic) with protection (the bandage) in one step.

FAMOUS FATHER AT WORK

Johnson & Johnson's first scientific director was Frederick B. Kilmer, who capably served the company for 45 years, beginning in 1888, and was instrumental in its early success in creating the surgical dressing industry. Fred Kilmer was the father of Joyce Kilmer, the poet-hero of World War I.

PHARMACEUTICAL FIRSTS

When Edward R. Squibb established his pharmaceutical practice in New Brunswick in 1858, he started New Jersey on its journey to becoming the country's leading location for innovative medical laboratories. It was Dr. Squibb who made a new anesthetic—ether—available to the medical profession, before the Civil War.

Along with Squibb Institute for Medical Research, Johnson & Johnson, Merck Laboratories, Schering Company, Hoffman-LaRoche Applied Research Laboratories, Carter-Wallace, and Ciba Pharmaceutial Company are among the larger and better-known companies to establish facilities in New Jersey—making the state the pharmaceutical industry's equivalent of the computer industry's Silicon Valley. The presence of so many outstanding research and development–oriented, health-related companies gave New Jersey a prominent role in many pharmaceutical firsts. Consider these:

- Merck Laboratories in Rahway, Union County, with scientist J. M. Sprague heading the research in 1939, was the first to synthesize the group of sulfas called sulfapyrimidines, a key development in the advancement of early chemotherapy.

- England's Alexander Fleming discovered penicillin and its impact, but it was the Squibb Institute for Medical Research in New Brunswick that received the first Fleming culture in 1941 and was the first to produce penicillin in fermentation tanks, an early step toward mass production of the invaluable drug.

- Lewis H. Sarett, a 26-year-old Merck scientist, in 1944 was the first to synthesize the human hormone cortisone, creating a drug that helped rheumatoid arthritics cope with the debilitating effects of their disease. Cortisone changes internal tissues so that they become resistant to stress, injury, or disease. Synthetic cortisone has also been used successfully for treating allergies, skin diseases, and asthma.

- It was the Schering Company of Bloomfield, Essex County, that in 1955 began large-quantity production of synthetic cortisone, which is five times as potent as unaltered cortisone.

- Dr. Robert Williams, who lived in Roselle, Union County, discovered vitamin B-1 in 1910 when he saved an infant dying of beri-beri in the

Philippines by administering a few drops of rice bran syrup. In 1934, he invented a process to produce the vitamin synthetically. Working with Williams was his son-in-law, Robert Waterman, who later became research director for Schering.

- Merck Labs helped Williams with the synthesis of vitamin B-1 and also discovered vitamin E. The company's biggest contribution in the field of vitamins, however, was the isolation and synthesis of vitamin B-12 in 1947. Relatively inexpensive to mass-produce, B-12 is added to animal foods.

- Selman A. Waksman, a professor of microbiology at Rutgers University in New Brunswick, received the 1952 Nobel Prize in physiology and medicine for his 1943 discovery of streptomycin, a bacteria-fighting drug that saved lives by successfully treating tuberculosis, dysentery, and whooping cough, all of which had proven resistant to penicillin. (Waksman openly credits Merck for its help and support in isolating, purifying, manufacturing, and testing streptomycin.) Today, the Waksman Institute of Microbiology is a free-standing research facility on the Busch campus of Rutgers University.

- In 1953, the Ciba Pharmaceutical Company in Summit, Union County, developed the antihypertensive drug Serpasil and coined the word "tranquilizer" because of the product's calming effect. The company also developed Ritalin, one of the first stimulant drugs, which is now widely prescribed for the treatment of Attention Deficit Disorder (ADD).

VALIUM

During the turbulent 1960s, Leo H. Sternbach provided a soothing antidote for millions of Americans. A chemist for the Hoffmann-La Roche Pharmaceutical Company in Nutley, Essex County, Sternbach discovered what became known as Librium, a drug that depressed portions of the central nervous system without making users sleepy.

Sternbach and his assistant, Earl Reeder, continued their research at the urging of the company. In 1959, the two men found diazepam, a compound without the bitter taste of Librium that was also 5 to 10 times more powerful so that it could be taken in smaller doses. The drug would become known as Valium, from the Latin word meaning to be strong and well.

A Bestseller

Introduced to consumers in 1963, Valium became a part of popular culture. The Rolling Stones sang about it in their 1966 hit "Mother's Little Helper." The mellowness induced by Valium led doctors to prescribe it for everything from aching backs to anxiety attacks. A dozen years after its introduction, more than 60 million prescriptions for Valium were being written annually, making it the top-selling prescription drug in the country.

Celebrity revelations about Valium—Elvis Presley had it in his system when he died and First Lady Betty Ford disclosed she mixed it with her cocktails—combined with an exposé of the drug on the television program *60 Minutes*, led to a reduction in its use. Others claimed it caused sleeping, eating, and panic disorders. Sternbach defended Valium, saying it worked fine if taken in the proper dosage.

Hoffmann-La Roche continues to make Valium, but sales in the 1990s are just a fraction of what they were during the peak years of the 1970s.

OTHER STERNBACH DISCOVERIES

Leo Sternbach also discovered the first commercially feasible synthesis of the vitamin biotin and the synthesis of the antispasmodics Quarzan and Librax, used to treat peptic ulcers. He holds more than 230 patents. Sternbach was a charter member of the New Jersey Inventors Hall of Fame in 1989.

Games People Play

ORGANIZED BASEBALL

Baseball is known as the national pastime, but the roots of the sport lie in New Jersey, where the first baseball game featuring two teams with nine men on a side and the first box score was played on June 19, 1846.

The game between a pair of New York City teams—the Knickerbockers and the New York Nine—was played on the Elysian Fields of Hoboken. With playing fields at a premium in New York because of increased development, North Jersey offered plenty of space for a baseball game.

The two teams took the Stevens-Barclay Ferry across the Hudson River to Hoboken for their historic game. The New York Nine easily won by the score of 23-1. In a display of good sportsmanship, the losing team treated the winners to a banquet.

Baseball evolved from two British games: cricket, which was divided into innings and supervised by umpires, and rounders, a children's game played with a stick and a ball. Cricket and rounders were brought to the United States by early colonists.

The Knickerbockers had been organized on September 23, 1845, as the New York Knickerbocker Baseball Club under the direction of Alexander Cartwright, who would serve as the umpire for the first game. Cartwright was instrumental in introducing the rules that would be carried over into the modern game of baseball. Foul lines were introduced and the balk (an attempt by the pitcher to deceive the runner) was prohibited. A batter got three missed swings before being declared out. Runners had to be tagged with the ball, rather than struck with a thrown ball, in order for an out to be recorded. This rule paved the way for the introduction of the hard ball that made modern baseball the sport it is today.

The Elysian Fields lived up to its dictionary definition of "happy, blissful or delightful," with its picnic grove for fans and nearby taverns for players to retire to after the game. A plaque in the shape of a baseball diamond has been installed at the Hoboken site, now a defunct Maxwell House coffee plant at 11th and Washington Streets. It reads:

> The seeds that led to organized baseball were planted on Elysian Fields [in] Hoboken, New Jersey, June 19, 1846. The rules were established by Alexander J. Cartwright, who umpired the game in which the Knickerbockers were defeated by the New York Nine, 23-1.

More Baseball Notes

New Jersey never has had a major league team of its own, but it was used as a spring training site by three major league teams during the 1940s. To cut down on travel during World War II, Baseball Commissioner Kenesaw Mountain Landis ordered major league teams to hold spring training at sites east of the Mississippi River and north of the Potomac River.

In 1943, the New York Yankees held spring training in Asbury Park, Monmouth County, and moved south to Atlantic City in 1944 and 1945. The New York Giants held spring training in Lakewood, Ocean County, from 1943 to 1945. The Boston Red Sox came to Pleasantville, Atlantic County, for one spring training season in 1945.

The Brooklyn Dodgers played 15 "home" games at Roosevelt Stadium in Jersey City, Hudson County, in 1956 and 1957 because of what the team considered to be inadequate playing conditions at Ebbets Field in Brooklyn. In retrospect, it was a rehearsal for the Dodgers' move to Los Angeles for the start of the 1958 season.

"From small things, mama, big things one day come," sang New Jersey native Bruce Springsteen. He was singing about romance, but the subject matter of his song could have been college football.

The sport that writer Dan Jenkins once dubbed "Saturday's America" is now played from coast to coast before packed stadiums and national television audiences. College football got its modest start in New Brunswick, Middlesex County, on November 6, 1869, when Rutgers University and Princeton University played the first intercollegiate football game. Rutgers defeated Princeton, 6-4, in a game played on a parcel of ground where the current Rutgers gymnasium now stands. A crowd of about 100 people turned out to watch the historic game.

This monument at Rutgers University in New Brunswick commemorates the first college football game, played on November 6, 1869, between Rutgers University and Princeton University. *Courtesy of Rutgers University*

Athletic Rivals

The two universities, located only 20 miles apart, were natural rivals. In 1869, Princeton had defeated Rutgers in baseball by the lopsided score of 40-2. "Rutgers longed for a chance to square things," said John W. Herbert, a member of the Rutgers Class of 1872, who played in the first game. Rutgers issued a challenge to Princeton in football in an attempt to salve its wounded pride.

The game was played with two teams of 25 men each, using rugby-like regulations. Each team stationed two men near the opponent's goal in hopes of getting an easy score. The other 23 players were split into groups of 11 and 12. While the 11 so-called fielders stayed in their own territory and played defense, the other 12, dubbed "bulldogs," played offense. Under the rules the two sides agreed upon, each score represented a "game" and 10 games would complete a contest. After each score, the opponents changed direction, as football teams do today after each half. The ball could be advanced only by hitting or kicking it with the feet, hands, head, or sides.

Playing the Game

The game was noteworthy for the Rutgers squad's introduction of the flying wedge, a formation in which a team forms a group of blockers around an offensive man who advances the ball down the field, a technique used on kickoff returns by modern-day football teams. Similarly, Princeton has been credited with developing the concept of the blocking back, a player who leads the charge through the defense for the man controlling the ball. Both concepts would be refined as college football gained in popularity in the coming years.

The game was closely contested, with the score tied at 4-4 after the first eight games. A report of the game that appeared in the November 1869 issue of the *Targum*, Rutgers' undergraduate newspaper, said the game consisted of "headlong running, wild shouting and frantic kicking." Rutgers rallied to score the last two goals and clinch the victory, avenging its defeat in baseball. Princeton won the rematch between the two schools, but a third game was never played because of protests from educators at both institutions that the games were disrupting the players' studies. Despite the setback, Rutgers was able to recruit Columbia University to play during the 1870 season. College football had taken its first step toward becoming a national phenomenon.

COMMEMORATIVE STAMP ISSUED

In 1969, the U.S. Postal Service issued a commemorative stamp on the 100th anniversary of the first college football game.

GOLF TEE

Look back at the game of golf in the early 1920s and imagine golfers heading to the first hole. Once there, they wouldn't reach into their golf bag for a little wooden tee—such a thing didn't exist. Instead, golfers of the day would dip their hand into a bucket of water and form their tee out of a mound of sand.

Today's golf tee—that little wooden or plastic spike that so neatly holds the golf ball for drives—is one of those inventions that surely would have left golfers of the 1920s muttering, "Why didn't I think of that?"

William Lowell did think of that. A dentist from Maplewood, Essex County, Lowell wasn't quite satisfied with the hand-in-the-water-bucket, sand-mound tee. By using his dental tools, Lowell was able in 1921 to carve a golf tee out of wood and affix a small "cup" to hold the ball. Three years later, he held a patent on a seemingly simple, one-piece golf tee that would change the game.

The golf tee is an essential part of a golfer's equipment and has been used by such stars as (from left) Arnold Palmer, Gene Sarazen, and Jimmy Demaret. *Courtesy of the* Courier-Post

That change, however, did not occur overnight. In fact, Lowell's invention was initially scoffed at and may have never gained acceptance in the world of golf if not for some innovative marketing by Lowell and his sons. Recognizing that even professional golfers would not accept the tees as gifts, Lowell went so far as to pay $1,500 to the greatest golfer of the era, the legendary Walter Hagen, and to trick-shot artist Joe Kirkwood to use the tees during an exhibition tour. Wherever they played golf, Hagen and Kirkwood would leave tees behind for club members, and soon golfers were asking their pro shops where they could get more of them.

The marketing was successful, but Lowell's early estimate of sales suffered a blow because of an unexpected practice—golfers retrieved their tees after use. He had expected golfers to leave the tees behind after hitting their drives; in fact, the first 5,000 tees were green so they would blend in with the grass. Once aware that golfers would retain their tees, Lowell's company, Nieblo Manufacturing of New York, changed the color of the tees to red and called the product "Reddy Tees." The early tees were made of the finest white birch by a wood turner in Maine. Exhibits of golf tees are on display at the U.S. Golf Association Museum in Far Hills, Somerset County. Lowell was inducted into the New Jersey Inventors Hall of Fame in 1998.

☞ To Visit: U.S. Golf Association Museum and Library

The museum and library, also known as Golf House, are located off Route 512 between Interstate 287 and Interstate 78.
Far Hills, NJ 07931
Hours: Monday-Friday, 9 A.M.-5 P.M.; Saturday-Sunday, 10 A.M.-4 P.M.
Closed New Year's Day, Easter, Thanksgiving, and Christmas.
Admission free.
For more information, contact the U.S. Golf Association, P.O. Box 708, Far Hills, NJ 07931
908-234-2300; 908-234-9687 (fax)
www.usga.com

ANOTHER GOLF FIRST IN NEW JERSEY

As local legend has it, New Jersey was also instrumental in the development of the lingo of golf. The term *birdie*, which means one shot under par on a given hole, was reportedly first uttered by a group of golfers at the Atlantic City Country Club in the early 1900s. A plaque at the venerable club's old 12th hole, now a practice green, marks the spot where the phrase was first coined.

RADIO BROADCAST OF A BASEBALL GAME

Baseball, born in New Jersey, took a giant step toward reaching the masses when it hit the airwaves for the first time in 1921.

Game 1 of the 1921 World Series pitted the New York Yankees against the New York Giants on October 5. Both teams played their regular season games at the Polo Grounds, and even though neither team traveled for the World Series, the intra-city game was the first of what was dubbed the "Subway Series," since fans and players for both teams arrived at the stadium via the city's subway system. With so many fans of both teams within broadcast range of New York City, the game was conveniently suited for radio.

Capitalizing on this concentrated fan base, radio station WJZ of Newark, Essex County, took the steps necessary to air the game. Play-by-play bulletins were telephoned from the Polo Grounds to the radio station by Sandy Hunt, the sports editor of the *Sunday Call* newspaper in Newark. From the station, Tommy Cowan served as the relay man, providing the information to the station's listeners and effectively creating the first play-by-play broadcast of a game.

RADIO AND RUTH, PERFECT TOGETHER

The 1921 World Series broadcast was spurred in part by the sensational regular season of baseball's celebrity, the incomparable Babe Ruth. The Yankees' Ruth hit an incredible 59 home runs, in an era when home runs were hard to come by, and compiled a .378 batting average with 171 RBIs, 144 walks, and 177 runs.

PROFESSIONAL BASKETBALL CHAMPION

Think of professional basketball dynasties and several teams come to mind: the Boston Celtics of the late 1950s and 1960s, the Los Angeles Lakers of the 1980s, and the Chicago Bulls of the 1990s. The city of Trenton could stake a claim to being home to the very first basketball dynasty, as its team was the champion of the National League of Professional Basketball, the first such league, during the 1898-99 and 1899-1900 seasons.

The league consisted of three teams in New Jersey (Trenton Nationals, Mercer County; Millville Glassblowers, Cumberland County; and Camden Electrics, Camden County) and three teams in Philadelphia (Philadelphia Quakers, Germantown Athletic Association Nationals, and Kensington Hancock Athletic Association).

Besides winning the first professional basketball championship, the Trenton Nationals played in the first game against Kensington on December 1, 1898, at Textile Hall in Philadelphia, and posted the first victory, a 22-18 triumph.

This logo was created for the 100th anniversary of professional basketball. *Courtesy of Sports Nostalgia Research; logo created by Charlie McGill*

A Quiet Beginning

The popularity of basketball spread quietly after Dr. James Naismith invented the sport in 1891, explained Bill Himmelman of Sports Nostalgia Research in Norwood, Bergen County. Himmelman, the historian for the National Basketball Association, said the sporting press in Philadelphia began to lobby in print for the creation of a professional basketball league. Named after baseball's National League, the basketball league was organized in Philadelphia on July 30, 1898.

Playing rules were adopted and a schedule was drawn up. Teams played two 20-minute halves. There were no limits on personal fouls, as players could incur 10 to 12 fouls without worrying about fouling out. Players could get away with more indiscretions as there was only one referee working per game.

Scoring was at a premium as teams averaged between 16 and 24 points per game. Teams in the National Basketball Association routinely score more points in one quarter today. Al Cooper of Trenton was the leading scorer for the first season of the National League of Professional Basketball, averaging a modest 8.8 points per game. Trenton teammate Harry Stout was the runner-up for the scoring title, with an average of 6.9 points per game.

"A good field-goal shooting average was 12 percent, a good foul-shooting percentage was 50 percent," said Himmelman. A big part of the problems was with the equipment the players used. "The science of making a perfectly round ball was not there," Himmelman noted. "The balls varied in weight," he added, making it difficult for shooters to get a grip.

Teams played their home games in local armories or social clubs for such fraternal organizations as the Elks. The courts were surrounded by wire fences, and there was no out-of-bounds because a ball hitting the fence was considered in play. Because the fences more or less caged in the court, the first basketball players got the nickname "cagers." Attendance for the first season ranged from 500 to 2,000 people per game.

The Trenton Nationals were the dominant team in the league's first season, with a record of 18-2, finishing four games ahead of the second-place Millville Glassblowers, who had a record of 14-6.

New Name, but Repeat Champions

Change was a hallmark of the league's six-year history: franchises changed names, switched towns, or ceased operations. The Trenton Nationals were champions again in the 1899-1900 season, but the team's nickname was changed to the Trenton Tigers. The New York Gothamites and the Bristol Pile Drivers were the league champions in the third and fourth years, respectively, while the Camden Electrics were champions in the fifth and sixth seasons.

The National League of Professional Basketball disbanded after the 1903-04 season, but it laid the foundation for other professional leagues. Regional leagues sprang up in other sections of the country. The NBA would get its start after World War II and go on to prove that professional basketball could succeed and flourish on a national basis.

CHARTER MEMBER OF THE ABA

The Garden State had a charter franchise in the American Basketball Association, a league formed to challenge the NBA, for the 1967-68 season. In a throwback to the National League of Professional Basketball, the New Jersey Americans played their home games in the Teaneck Armory in Bergen County. The armory could hold 4,800 people, but attendance for the games was often less than 500. The Americans finished their first season with a record of 36-42, then moved to Long Island for the 1968-69 season.

New Jersey is not normally associated with horse country, but the Garden State has the distinction of hosting the first derby, a horse race for three-year-olds. The first running of the Jersey Derby was on June 7, 1864, in Paterson, Passaic County, 11 years before the first running of the Kentucky Derby. Sponsored by the Passaic County Agricultural Society, the race featured 12 of the nation's top three-year-olds in the mile-and-a-half competition.

The derby created an air of excitement during a troubling time. "When men met for business by day and assembled for amusement by night, the Derby, next to the [Civil] War and the state of the country, was the prevailing topic," claimed a report in the June 18, 1864, edition of *Spirit of the Times*.

Jockey Laffit Pincay, Jr. sits atop Spend a Buck before the 1985 Jersey Derby race at Garden State Park in Cherry Hill.
Courtesy of the Courier-Post

First and Later Winners

An estimated 10,000 fans, many of whom traveled by horse and carriage and the Erie Railroad, turned out to see the derby. Norfolk, a bright bay horse, won by 10 lengths over second-place finisher Tipperary.

The Jersey Derby went on a 78-year hiatus and would not be run again until 1942 at the original Garden State Park in what is now Cherry Hill, Camden County. The name of the race was changed to the Jersey Handicap.

One of the biggest races in the history of the event came in 1948. The race was then known as the Jersey Stakes. With legendary jockey Eddie Arcaro in the saddle, Citation, the winner of the Kentucky Derby and the Preakness, defeated four other rivals to win the Jersey Stakes by 11 lengths. Citation then went to New York and won the Belmont Stakes, completing the Triple Crown. He was the only horse to win the Triple Crown and Jersey Stakes in the same year.

Eugene Mori, owner of Garden State Park, restored the name Jersey Derby to the race in 1960. Bally Ache and jockey Bobby Ussery won it that year.

A Trip to Atlantic City

Fire destroyed Garden State Park on April 14, 1977, and the Atlantic City Race Course, in Hamilton, Atlantic County, was the host of five Jersey Derbies before the rebuilt Garden State Park reopened in 1985. The Jersey Derby returned with a flourish to Cherry Hill that year when Spend a Buck, winner of the Kentucky Derby, bypassed the Preakness to enter the Jersey Derby, forfeiting the chance to win the Triple Crown. Spend a Buck's owners got some financial consolation when the horse won the Jersey Derby, receiving the winner's share of $600,000 plus $2 million by sweeping a four-race series: the Cherry Hill Mile, Garden State Stakes, Kentucky Derby, and Jersey Derby.

The Jersey Derby continues to evolve. It was run on the grass and under lights for the first time in 1993.

MARBLES HALL OF FAME

The New Jersey shore conjures up a wide range of summertime associations, from the beach to the Boardwalk, from salt water taffy to surfing. Not as publicized are the shore's ties to the childhood game of marbles. For most of this century, Wildwood, Cape May County, has been host to the National Marbles Tournament, and it is the home of the National Marbles Hall of Fame, which opened there in June 1993.

George Ernst lines up a shot during a match in the 1986 marbles tournament in Wildwood. *Courtesy of the* Courier-Post

The beach in Wildwood provides the perfect summertime backdrop for the marbles competition in 1972. *Courtesy of the* Courier-Post

History of the Game

While the start of the tournament dates back to 1922 in Philadelphia, the game of marbles has a colorful history that starts before the birth of Christ. Children in ancient times played marbles using pebbles, fruit pits, and nuts. History has it that Roman emperor Augustus Caesar played marbles as a child, using nuts. Engraved marbles have been excavated from earthen mounds constructed by tribes of North American Indians before the first Europeans settled on the continent. And excavation of Stone Age tools in eastern Ireland revealed such items as marbles or balls averaging one to two times the diameter of contemporary ones.

The names and rules of marbles games are as varied as the locales where they are played. Games include taw (also called ringtaw or ringer), in which players attempt to shoot marbles out of a ring drawn on the ground. In pot games, a player can attempt to shoot his own marbles or his opponent's into a hole in the ground. In bridgeboard (also called nineholes), a board with several numbered arches is set up, and players attempt to shoot their marbles through the arches.

The Jersey Tourney

The game of marbles was quite popular with children in the early part of this century, and the marbles tournament was started to sustain a national interest in the game. The tournament has been held in New Jersey every summer since 1923, except for 1944 and 1945 during World War II. Wildwood hosted the tournament from 1937 to 1948 and then again from 1960 to 1975. Great Adventure theme park was the host in 1976, and the tournament was restored to Wildwood in 1977. It's been held there ever since. While New Jersey has been the host site of the marbles tournament since 1923, the state has never had a marbles champion of its own.

Ten cement rings set on pilings are permanently implanted in the sand on the beach at Wildwood Avenue in Wildwood. The competition area has been dubbed Ringer Stadium, named for the official game of the tournament. The game of ringer is played by placing 13 marbles in the form of a cross in a 10-foot circle with players alternating shots. The winner is the first player to shoot seven marbles out of the ring.

☞ To Visit: National Marbles Hall of Fame

The museum documents the history of the National Marbles Tournament, which has been held annually in Wildwood, with one exception, since 1960.

The National Marbles Hall of Fame, which occupies a room at the George F. Boyer Historical Museum in Wildwood, includes a list of the national champions, autographs, trophies, tournament shirts, and a history of the game.

National Marbles Hall of Fame
Spencer Avenue and Holly Beach Station Mall
Wildwood, NJ 08260
609-523-0277
Hours: May-September: daily, 10 A.M.-2 P.M.; October-April: Thursday-Sunday, 10 A.M.-2 P.M.

MARBLES SCHOLARSHIPS

Other New Jersey municipalities that have served as host of the marbles tournament are Atlantic City, Ocean City, and Asbury Park. Boys and girls ranging in age from 8 to 14 come from around the country to compete over a four-day period in June. Tournament winners receive a scholarship and are inducted into the National Marbles Hall of Fame.

LITTLE LEAGUE PERFECT GAME

Very few people outside of old Delaware Township—now known as Cherry Hill, Camden County—will recognize the name of Frederick Shapiro. But in 1956, the 12-year-old Shapiro needed less than two hours on a mound in central Pennsylvania to become a local legend.

Shapiro, the tallest player on the team, was the star pitcher on Delaware Township's all-star baseball team of 11- and 12-year-olds competing in the Little League World Series in Williamsport, Pennsylvania. The Delaware Township team was one of eight regional champions in the World Series

Frederick Shapiro holds a baseball autographed by members of the Delaware Township Little League team. He was honored by the Baseball Hall of Fame in Cooperstown, New York, for having pitched the first perfect game in the Little League World Series.
Courtesy of the Courier-Post

and had advanced to the semifinals following an exciting 9-8 quarterfinal win over Tuckahoe, New York.

In the semifinal game against a team from Colton, California, Shapiro took center stage. He pitched six flawless innings, retiring all 18 batters he faced to complete the first perfect game—no hits, no walks, and no errors by his team—in Little League World Series history and lead Delaware Township to a 2-0 victory and a berth in the Series final.

The Delaware Township team ultimately lost in the 1956 championship game, 3-1, to Roswell, New Mexico, and in doing so achieved another first for New Jersey—becoming the first team to finish as World Series runner-up in consecutive years. A year earlier, Frederick Shapiro and his teammates on the Delaware Township team had lost in the 1955 World Series finale to Morrisville, Pennsylvania. That game in itself marked a first when it took Morrisville seven innings to win, 4-3—the first extra-inning game in Little League World Series history. (A regulation Little League game is six innings.)

Shapiro's perfect game was topped a year later when Angel Macias of Monterrey, Mexico, became the first person to pitch a perfect game in the final game of a Little League World Series.

ANOTHER LITTLE LEAGUE FIRST

Little League baseball was founded in Williamsport, Pennsylvania, in 1939 and by 1946, only 12 leagues existed—all in Pennsylvania. New Jersey achieved another Little League first in 1947 when Hammonton, Atlantic County, formed the first Little League outside of Pennsylvania. By the time Delaware Township appeared in the World Series in 1955 and 1956, more than 4,000 leagues existed throughout North America.

Mad Scientists

THE FIRST TRANSISTOR

Some 50 years ago, William B. Shockley sent an understated note to some colleagues at Bell Telephone Laboratories in Murray Hill, Union County, inviting them to observe the demonstration of "some effects. I hope you can come."

This thumbnail-sized digital signal processor, the heart of Lucent Technologies' newest modem chipsets, contains 2.1 million transistors.
Courtesy of Lucent Technologies

The December 23, 1947, demonstration centered around an odd-looking device that resembled a piece of abstract sculpture or the insides of a light bulb, with an inverted triangle and pieces of metal from an old coat hanger jutting out at crooked angles. In reality, the contraption consisted of gold strips, insulators, wires, and germanium. Shockley, along with fellow physicists John Bardeen and Walter H. Brattain, would be demonstrating their invention of the transistor, a solid-state device for amplifying, controlling, and generating electrical signals.

The demonstration was simple and took less than 30 minutes; the transistor was used to amplify a voice signal over a loudspeaker. The implications were huge. The transistor and its descendants would render the vacuum tube—used to power early computers and television sets—obsolete. For example, the University of Pennsylvania's ENIAC computer, considered state of the art at the time, used 18,000 vacuum tubes, filled several large rooms, and consumed enough power to light 10 homes. The transistor would increase a computer's power while decreasing its size. The impact of the transistor was not evident at first glance. A half century later, that impact is unmistakable.

STAGGERING NUMBERS

Here's an example to illustrate the advantages of the transistor: If a typical cellular phone were made up of vacuum tubes, it would occupy a building slightly larger than the Washington Monument. There are approximately 200 million billion transistors in the world today—about 40 million for every man, woman, and child, according to Lucent Technologies. The cost of producing a transistor has gone from $45 in the 1950s to less than one-thousandth of a cent today.

"Without the transistor, you would be perpetually in the '50s," said John Schmalzel, chairman of the Engineering Department at Rowan University in Glassboro. "I don't see how modern society would have advanced past that decade."

Today, transistors are as ubiquitous as grains of sand on the Jersey shore. More than half a billion are manufactured every second. The transistor's impact on modern electronics and communications has been far-reaching, from the inner ear to outer space, from the moon landing to microsurgery. Personal computers, modems, fax machines, cellular phones, cable television, compact disc players, ATM banking, and touch-tone calling—all practically indispensable—wouldn't exist without the transistor. Neither would hearing aids, pacemakers, electrocardiograms, and CAT scans.

The transistor's invention sparked a revolution in solid-state physics as it laid the foundation for more advanced applications, such as integrated circuits which use more than one transistor. The work at Bell Labs would lead to New Jersey's nickname as "The Research Center of the World."

THE BIRTH OF TEFLON

His name is largely forgotten by most cooks and chefs—if it was ever known at all. When it comes to culinary achievements, though, Dr. Roy Plunkett can stand alongside such luminaries as Julia Child, James Beard, and Paul Prudhomme.

Plunkett's breakthrough—the discovery of Teflon—didn't come while he was laboring over a hot stove in his kitchen. It occurred by accident at Jackson Laboratory, a division of DuPont's Chambers Works in Deepwater, Salem County, on April 6, 1938. The 27-year-old scientist and Jack Relak, his laboratory assistant, were doing research on a new refrigerant. The two men were part of a group of scientists studying all aspects of fluorinated hydrocarbons.

Relak withdrew a cylinder of Freon from a dry ice storage bin and opened it, but nothing came out. However, the cylinder still weighed as

Roy Plunkett discovered Teflon in his laboratory at DuPont's Chambers Works plant in Deepwater in 1938.
Courtesy of the Courier-Post

much as it would have had it still contained Freon. Plunkett sliced the cylinder open and discovered the insides were coated with "a white, solid material which was supposed to be a polymerized product of the Freon compound," as he wrote in his laboratory notebook. Because its chemical composition was unknown, the new product was issued a laboratory code number: K. 416. The unsuccessful refrigeration experiment would turn into one of the great success stories of the 20th century.

The white, waxy substance was dubbed tetrafluoroethylene (PTFE), better known now by its trademark name of Teflon. Today, Teflon-coated pots, pans, cookie sheets, and muffin tins are found in kitchens around the world, preventing food from sticking to the surface of cookware. Nearly four in five of the pots and pans sold in the United States are coated with Teflon or one of its chemical cousins, according to industry estimates.

The substance Plunkett discovered had some amazing characteristics. Teflon's qualities include a complete indifference to attack by any and all chemicals. It retains its physical properties over a wide range of temperatures, from 450° to 725°F. Heat is able to pass through Teflon without melting it. The ingredient, known as the world's most slippery solid, holds together in a vacuum, making it invaluable for use in outer space.

From the Moon to the Mob

Teflon's uses go far beyond the kitchen. As a matter of fact, they're out of this world. Teflon was an essential part of the technology that allowed man to walk on the moon. The material coated the outer layers of space suits and lined the systems used to carry liquid oxygen during the Apollo flights of the late 1960s and early 1970s. Other uses for Teflon in space included heat-shields for rocket re-entry and wire insulation.

In 1976, Robert Gore discovered that a piece of stretched Teflon had tiny holes big enough to let water vapor out but too small to allow water droplets in. He applied the Teflon to fabric and called it Gore-Tex, the first breathable waterproof clothing.

Teflon's amazing characteristics served to make it one of the most valuable and versatile substances ever discovered, contributing to significant advances in such areas as aerospace, communications, electronics, industrial processes, and architecture. Teflon coats electrical wires, chemical tanks, jogging suits, and light bulbs. It's been used as a corrosion insulator

SLIPPERY RON

Teflon's slippery nature even changed the English language. Former Colorado congresswoman Pat Schroeder dubbed President Reagan the "Teflon president" in 1983 for his ability to avoid blame for problems in his administration. New York Mob boss John Gotti was known as the "Teflon don" for evading the law several times before he was finally convicted.

between the copper skin and inner stainless steel framework of the Statue of Liberty, and as a coating for the 10-acre Fiberglass roof of the Silverdome in Pontiac, Michigan.

All of this was far from Plunkett's mind in 1938. A resident of Woodstown, Salem County, Plunkett was only two years out of graduate school (he received a doctorate in chemistry from Ohio State University) when he made his discovery. "If there was any luck involved in the discovery," Plunkett once observed, "probably part of it was that we didn't get blown up."

Plunkett died of cancer on May 12, 1994, leaving a legacy of involvement that "is as important to modern society as the light bulb, telephone and automobile," one DuPont executive said in 1988. Plunkett realized new uses for Teflon would continue to be discovered well into the 21st century when he said, "The uses of Teflon are limited only by the imagination."

BELL LABS: TOUCH-TONE DIALING AND MORE

When it comes to New Jersey firsts, Bell Laboratories is in a class by itself. Based in Murray Hill, Union County, Bell Labs (the research and development unit of Lucent Technologies, a spin-off of AT&T) has received more than 26,000 patents, averaging one a day since the company's founding in 1926. Since the issuance of a patent is in fact a designation of a "first," Bell Labs' creations and innovations could fill this entire book.

Bell Labs' incredible timeline of firsts includes sound motion pictures (1926), the artificial larynx (1929), stereophonic sound (1933), the invaluable transistor (1947), direct long-distance dialing (1951), the solar battery (1954), the laser (1958), the first orbiting international communications satellite— Telstar (1962), the UNIX software system (1969), C++ computer language (1983), and the first transatlantic fiber-optic cable (1988), to name just a few.

Many of Bell's "firsts" serve as building blocks to a wealth of invaluable products and services. It was, in fact, the transistor that led to one of Bell's most visible and consumer-friendly breakthroughs in 1964—the touch-tone telephone.

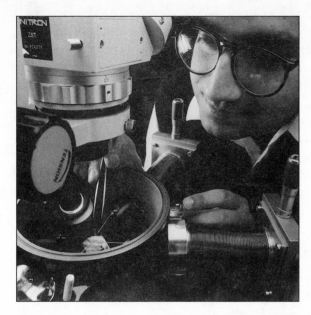

Ananth Dodabalapur of the Bell Labs optical physics department in Murray Hill helped to invent low-cost "plastic" transistors that can be printed cheaply on sheets of plastic, much the same way books are printed on paper. *Photo by Dave Hoffman, courtesy of Lucent Technologies*

SNEAK PREVIEW

The first touch-tone system, which used tones in the voice frequency range rather than pulses generated by rotary dials, was actually used by telephone operators in a central switching office in Baltimore as early as 1941. It was considered much too expensive, however, for general consumer use.

Bell Labs' personnel, always looking for greater efficiency in existing products, were intrigued by touch-tone because it increased the speed of dialing. As the cost of transistors and associated circuit components decreased, the viability of touch-tone service in home telephones increased.

With the cost-effective technical components in place in the early 1960s, Bell took the next step—it considered human elements in designing the touch-tone phone. Why, for example, weren't the touch-tone buttons simply placed in the corresponding circle locations of the existing rotary dial phones? According to Bell, "extensive human factor tests" determined the placement of the 0 to 9 buttons to limit dialing errors and increase dialing speed. The 10 number buttons were placed as they appear today, with the 11th and 12th buttons (# and *) later added to the right and left sides of the 0 in order to provide additional custom-calling features controlled by software in communications networks.

TOUCH-TONE'S PUBLIC DEBUT

The first commercial touch-tone phones were introduced during a well-received preview at the 1962 World's Fair in Seattle and were a hit with consumers when put on the market in 1964.

Bell Labs Does It Again, and Again, and...

Here are some more notable firsts from Bell:

- Live television transmission, 1927: Live images of Herbert Hoover are sent from Washington, D.C., to New York City via telephone lines.
- Speech synthesis, 1936: The first speech synthesis machine that re-creates human speech is publicly demonstrated.
- High-definition digital television (HDTV), 1989: Bell Labs develops video compression algorithms that point the way toward next-generation HDTV systems.
- elemedia, 1996: Breakthrough software technology that delivers telephone-quality voice and CD-quality music to customers using the Internet.

All of us have witnessed technological advances during our lifetime that have a dramatic impact on the way we live. Thomas Edison not only saw such advances during his incredible life (1847-1931), he was personally responsible for many of them—making New Jersey the birthplace of a true technological revolution.

The life and inventions of the "Wizard of Menlo Park" have been the subject of many books. Some four to five million pages of Edison's notes will ultimately be catalogued and computerized—an overwhelming task yet to be completed nearly 70 years after his death. Obviously, then, we can't mention here all that he accomplished during more than 60 years of research in Newark, Menlo Park, and West Orange, Essex County. Thomas Edison, recognized as the pioneer of technological teamwork, would likely have little problem with our hitting just the highlights of his "firsts." So here goes.

The Invention Factory

Edison first set up shop in 1870 in Newark, using funds obtained from the sale of his first money-making invention—the stock market ticker, which was based on telegraph technology invented by Samuel F. B. Morse 12 years before Edison was born. Six years later, Edison established his Menlo Park "invention factory," promising a new invention every 10 days and a major invention every six months. His first invention at Menlo Park amplified the volume of voices during a telephone conversation, vastly improving Alexander Graham Bell's telephone so that users would not have to shout to speak to one another.

Menlo Park was in fact a first itself. It marked the first time a business was created purely for research and development of new products. Today, such R&D companies are commonplace in California's Silicon Valley and other technology hotbeds. Menlo Park was also the site of Edison's most far-reaching inventions—the phonograph in 1877 and the electric light in

1879. The phonograph, then referred to as the talking machine, was Edison's favorite invention and was by his own admission invented by accident through his work on telegraphs and telephones. The first words recorded were "Mary had a little lamb." Ten years later, the machine was marketed to the public.

Seeing the Light

In his efforts to invent the incandescent light, Edison partnered in 1876 with New York millionaires J. P. Morgan and Cornelius Vanderbilt to form

Thomas Edison holds an experimental light bulb, called the Edison Effect lamp, in this 1919 photograph.
Courtesy of the Courier-Post

the Edison Electric Light Company, which is now General Electric. Three years, $40,000, and 1,200 experiments later, Edison did it—he invented a safe, mild, and inexpensive light to replace the candles and gaslights then in use in homes. His first bulbs were installed on the steamship *Columbia* and later in a New York City factory. In 1882, Edison invented a system to supply many lamps with electricity all at the same time, and he established the world's first electric light power station in lower Manhattan.

One of Edison's engineers, William J. Hammer, made a monumental discovery in 1883 that eventually led to the development of the electron tube, the forefather of electronics as we now know it. Without what was patented as the "Edison Effect," such commonplace electronic devices as radios, televisions, and computers would not have been developed.

Thomas Edison adjusts the focus on an early motion picture projector in his laboratory in this 1897 photograph.
Courtesy of the Courier-Post

Bigger and Better in West Orange

Edison's Menlo Park facility was in use for 10 years and was followed in 1887 by a new site in West Orange. The West Orange Edison Laboratory, which was 10 times bigger than the first lab in Menlo Park, comprised 14 buildings and employed more than 5,000 people. Out of the West Orange labs came such inventions or improvements as the motion picture camera (which, when coupled with the phonograph, led to the first talking pictures in 1913), the copy machine, the dictating machine, a cement mixer, the microphone, and the concept of film reels for motion picture cameras.

A MINUTE OF TRIBUTE

Three days after Edison died in 1931 at the age of 84, electric lights were dimmed for one minute throughout the United States as a tribute.

☞ To Visit: Edison National Historic Site

Edison's home, Glenmont, was built in 1880 in Llewellyn Park, one-half mile from the West Orange complex. The 29-room mansion contains original items used by the Edison family. The home and the lab complex are part of the Edison National Historic Site. Together they house 400,000 pieces, including many of Edison's inventions, such as the first phonograph.

Edison National Historic Site
Main Street and Lakeside Avenue
West Orange, NJ 07052
973-736-0550; 973-736-8496 (fax); 973-243-9122 (TDD)

Hours: The lab site is open daily except Thanksgiving, Christmas, and New Year's Day, 9 A.M.-5 P.M. Guided tours are hourly on the half-hour. Glenmont is open Wednesday to Sunday.
Admission $2; children under 17 are admitted free.

SOME WELL-KNOWN PARTNERS

Thomas Edison was called a genius, even by his contemporaries. But he insisted that "genius is one percent inspiration and 99 percent perspiration" and that "genius is hard work, stick-to-itiveness and common-sense." Genius is also surrounding yourself with the likes of Henry Ford, who worked at an Edison lab before setting up his car-making factory; George Eastman, who worked with Edison to make film strips and went on to be a partner in a little company now known as Kodak; and Harvey Firestone, who worked with Ford and Edison to make better rubber for car tires.

SUCCESSFUL NAVAL SUBMARINE

To claim to have developed a submarine can be a very shallow contention. The key, John Phillip Holland proved, was to make a *successful* submarine—one that, of course, could consistently return to the surface of the water under its own power, with all life and property inside intact.

Holland, an Irish music teacher, was at work developing such a practical submarine as early as the 1860s. He left Ireland in 1873 and settled in Paterson, Passaic County. He attempted to interest the U.S. Navy in a submarine as early as 1875, but was unsuccessful. Undaunted, he continued his work with the backing of the Fenian Society, a group of Irish patriots intent on diluting England's naval power. Holland's first submarine failed in 1878. Failure of a submarine is obviously a serious deterrent to potential buyers, and the U.S. Navy shied away from Holland's vessels for almost two decades. Finally, Holland convinced them of his submarine's potential seaworthiness and was commissioned in 1895 to build the Navy's first submarine.

Submarine No. 1

The *Holland* was launched in 1898 and proved capable of traveling under water for hours at a time, making it a serious threat as a naval weapon. The boat was powered under the water by a 60-cell battery and along the surface by a gasoline engine, which also served to recharge the battery. The submarine's weaponry consisted of self-propelled Whitehead torpedoes. The U.S. Navy purchased the ship in 1900 and commissioned it as the USS *Holland*, also known as Submarine No. 1. (For good measure, Holland also invented a respirator that would help the crew of the submarine escape in the event of catastrophe.)

The basic technology behind the USS *Holland*—submersion by flooding of ballast tanks and resurfacing by replacing the water in the ballast tanks with compressed air—remained intact through two world wars, although the volatile gasoline was replaced by safer diesel fuel as early as 1911.

HOLLAND'S BUSINESS WAS BOOMING

In the early 1900s, with the first world war on the horizon, the submarine business was booming for John Holland and competitor Simon Lake, an American inventor. Submarines designed by Holland not only found their way into the U.S. Navy but were also used by Russia and Japan. And even though he was originally backed financially by the Irish Fenian Society, which was intent on weakening England's strong navy, Holland broke ranks from the Society and sold submarines to Britain as well.

Nuclear-powered submarines replaced the diesel-driven ships in the U.S. Navy, beginning in 1954 with the launch of the USS *Nautilus*. That submarine sailed more than 100,000 miles without refueling; 90,000 of those miles were spent submerged.

THE BAR CODE

It's an inescapable part of the retail industry, found on items ranging from cereal boxes to compact discs, from books to magazines. The bar code, a set of black lines with a string of accompanying numbers, changed American business and was the brainchild of N. Joseph Woodland, a native of Atlantic City, Atlantic County. Woodland's universal code has become a standard fixture in the retail world, enabling cash register scanners to identify an item and its price almost instantly.

Working with colleague Bernard Silver, the self-employed Woodland received a patent for his Classifying Apparatus and Method in October 1952. The Universal Price Code identifies a product through its series of black lines, which come in varying lengths and widths.

Honored for His Work

Woodland sold the rights to his invention to Philco, but he later went to work for IBM. From 1971 to 1982, Woodland was responsible for developing IBM's Universal Price Code proposal and selling the concept to the grocery industry, where it is the accepted practice today. The bar code replaced the need to stamp an individual price on each product in the store (much to the chagrin of shoppers who often, it seems, aren't able to find a price tag that's readable by human eyes).

In 1992, Woodland received the National Medal of Technology from President George Bush for his invention and his contribution of bar code technology, which improved productivity in every industrial sector and triggered the rise of the bar code industry. The award presentation came after Bush, running for re-election, encountered a scanner in the supermarket and admitted he didn't know how it worked. Woodland was admitted to the New Jersey Inventors Hall of Fame in 1996.

MAN OF MANY TALENTS

Before inventing the bar code, Joseph Woodland worked on the U.S. Army's Manhattan Project in Oak Ridge, Tennessee, which led to the development of the atomic bomb during World War II.

THE TELEGRAPH

Batman had Robin. Johnny Carson had Ed McMahon. And Samuel F. B. Morse, widely recognized as the inventor of the telegraph, had his own sidekick, Alfred Vail.

Morse conceived of the electromagnetic telegraph in 1832 and unveiled a rough version of his invention in New York City in 1837. Vail was in the audience during that demonstration and watched as an electrical signal caused an electromagnet to activate a pen that marked lines on a moving paper tape.

Morse was a fine arts professor at New York University and founder of the National Academy of Design. Recognizing both mechanical and financial limitations, he brought Vail and his technical expertise into a partnership that would perfect the telegraph and revolutionize the communications industry.

Financial Backing

Vail arranged to have his father, Stephen, finance the work needed to improve the telegraph, and Morse and Vail set up shop in Stephen Vail's successful ironworks on Speedwell Avenue in Morristown, Morris County. Alfred Vail helped make several improvements to the primitive telegraph and was in part responsible for replacing an unwieldy code scheme utilized by the early telegraph with the dots and dashes of what is now known as Morse code.

A new and improved telegraph was demonstrated on January 6, 1838, when the partners looped three miles of wire around a room in the Morristown factory. Vail transmitted and Morse received the message: "A patient waiter is no loser." It was the first successful telegraph transmission, and it led to additional demonstrations. Ultimately, Congress approved $30,000 in funding for an experimental telegraph line between Washington, D.C., and Baltimore. In 1844, that wire carried the now infamous message, "What hath God wrought?" and essentially jump-started the telegraph business.

Within 10 years, 23,000 miles of wire crisscrossed the country, enabling the telegraph to play a large role in the development of the West, in the advancement of business, and even in improvements in railroad travel (it enabled trains and signalmen to communicate more easily with each other). Vail, however, lost interest in playing a further role in the industry and ultimately had no share in the business when it turned lucrative in the late 19th century. Morse, on the other hand, continued to patent the improved telegraph and eventually prospered greatly from this invention—offsetting his earlier disappointment when his inventions of water pumps and marble-carving machines proved to be commercial failures.

☞ To Visit: Historic Speedwell Museum

Historic Speedwell preserves the country estate of Stephen Vail, with its eight museum buildings. Exhibits highlight the Vail family's work in machine production, steam-powered transportation, and telegraphic communication. The Main Carriage House contains the exhibit "The Speedwell Ironworks: A History of Workers and Work" and covers the history of the ironworks. Much of the machinery for the SS *Savannah*, the first steamship to complete a transatlantic voyage in 1819, was produced at the ironworks.

Historic Speedwell Museum
333 Speedwell Avenue
Morristown, NJ 07960
973-540-0211
www.speedwell.org
Hours: May-October: Thursday-Friday, 12-4 P.M.; Saturday-Sunday, 1-5 P.M.
Admission charged.

Incredible Edibles

CANNED SOUP—AS WE KNOW IT TODAY

Think of Campbell Soup and a line of successful products comes to mind: Pepperidge Farm breads and cookies, Swanson frozen dinners, and, of course, such standbys as canned chicken noodle and tomato soups. But the Joseph Campbell Preserve Company, as it was known in 1869 when it was founded, has more than a prominent place in our kitchen cabinets. It has a significant place in history.

The company's turning point came in 1897 when Dr. John T. Dorrance—then working for the company for $7.50 per week—developed a formula for condensed soup. By halving the quantity of the heaviest ingredient in the soup (water) and producing a good-tasting, economically priced product, Dorrance laid the foundation for the company's success: canned, condensed soups.

In 1897, the company produced 10 cases of soup per week from its Camden, Camden County, factory. Eight years later, in 1905, soup production had soared to 20 million cans annually. The original five varieties—Tomato, Consommé, Vegetable, Chicken, and Oxtail—were instant hits with families who could enjoy high-quality soup in a fraction of the time it would take to make it from scratch. Soup sales became so strong that the company changed its name to the Campbell Soup Company in 1921. Today, some 2.5 billion cans of soup are sold in the United States each year. That's 70 cans per second.

The company's most popular soup, Chicken Noodle, was introduced in 1934 as Chicken with Noodles. Sales of the soup were lagging until

Condensed soup, produced by the Campbell Soup Company, quickly caught on in popularity. More than 16 million cans were sold in the United States in 1904, according to this advertisement that appeared in *Good Housekeeping* magazine in 1905. *Courtesy of the* Courier-Post

Freeman Gosden, an actor who portrayed Amos on the *Amos and Andy* radio show, misread an advertisement for the soup, calling it Chicken Noodle. The company received so many orders for the soup that the name was officially changed. Cream of Mushroom was introduced the same year and is the company's second-leading seller. One of the company's original condensed soups, Tomato, remains a bestseller more than 100 years after its introduction in 1897. Cream of Chicken (1947) and Vegetable Beef (1918) round out the top five leading sellers for the company.

MOSTLY HITS, A FEW MISSES

While Camden-based Campbell Soup Company has a long list of culinary successes, not every product the company has introduced during its 125-year history has been an instant hit with finicky consumers. Consider a few of Campbell's less popular products: FR-8, a version of the successful V8 juice that used fruit instead of vegetables; Liver Baby Soup; Black Cherry Soup; and Prune Soup with Oranges and Apricots.

FROZEN FRUITS AND VEGETABLES FOR MASS CONSUMPTION

Seabrook Farms in Upper Deerfield Township, Cumberland County, changed the eating habits of a nation by becoming the first company to freeze fruits and vegetables for mass consumption. Seabrook, located on more than 20,000 acres of land in Cumberland, Salem, Atlantic, and Gloucester Counties, employed about 5,000 workers, making it the largest vegetable farm in the world in the years right after World War II.

The company's innovations included scientifically scheduled planting and harvesting of crops and an overhead, movable system of irrigation. The mass quick-freezing of packaged fruits and vegetables is credited with introducing Americans to the frozen food section of the supermarket. The company's experiments with frozen foods began as early as 1913. In the 1930s, the company teamed up with Birdseye for quick-freezing fruits and vegetables in retail packages, using steam-powered ammonia compressors formerly used to make ice.

It is no exaggeration to say that Seabrook put the garden in the Garden State. At its commercial peak in the 1950s, the company helped satisfy a nation's appetite by producing 15 percent of the country's output of frozen vegetables. In 1954, for example, the production of asparagus equaled one serving for every resident of New York, Florida, Washington, and Texas combined.

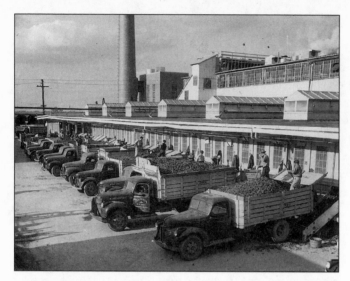

Truckloads of spinach are dumped into sorting lines at Seabrook Farms in the early 1950s. The spinach is sorted, blanched, drained, and packed into retail or institutional packages, according to quality.
Courtesy of the Seabrook Educational and Cultural Center

The guiding force behind the operation was Charles F. Seabrook, whose father, Arthur, launched the family's agricultural empire when he began farming on 61 acres in Deerfield Township in 1893. Charles displayed an early aptitude for farming when, in 1895, at the age of 14, he began experimenting with overhead irrigation and found that it increased celery production by as much as 300 percent. By 1912, the younger Seabrook took over management of the farm. He introduced industrial techniques—such as assembly lines and product research—into the business of farming. That led *Fortune* magazine to dub him "The Henry Ford of Agriculture" in the 1920s.

Quick Freezing

Seabrook Farms got a major boost during the 1930s with the quick freezing of its products. The technique of preserving produce meant a longer shelf life for fruits and vegetables and an expanded market for Seabrook products. Quick-freezing relied on a technological approach to increase crop production. The process also relied on quick work by employees. In some cases, less than an hour would elapse from the time a vegetable was harvested, washed, and then frozen at the company's 23-acre processing plant. In its peak years after World War II, Seabrook Farms would produce nearly two dozen types of vegetables (from asparagus to wax beans) and fruits (from apples to strawberries), shipped throughout the states east of the Mississippi River.

The sale of Seabrook Farms to Seaman Brothers in 1959 was the beginning of the end of an era. Fierce competition in the food industry led to the company's demise. Seabrook's fortunes went into decline in the 1970s, and the workforce had dropped to under 100 employees when the company closed its doors in March 1982. But the Seabrook name has not disappeared from food production. The new company of Seabrook Brothers and Sons began operating in 1977. The company was able to buy back the name of Seabrook Farms, 35 years after it was sold. The company's old slogan—"We grow our own so we know what's good and we freeze it right on the spot"—was applicable once again as the next generation of Seabrooks writes a new chapter in the family's agricultural history.

DOING CARTWHEELS AT SEABROOK

In a January 1955 article, *Life* magazine called Seabrook Farms "the biggest vegetable factory on earth." Seabrook Farms had a workforce that resembled a smaller version of the United Nations. In the years during and after World War II, Seabrook Farms had employees from more than 30 countries on four different continents, speaking in excess of two dozen languages. To demonstrate the economic power of Seabrook Farms, Charles F. Seabrook paid over 3,000 workers in silver dollars in June 1950. More than 250,000 silver dollars were brought in by armored truck for the "Cavalcade of Cartwheels." Back then, *cartwheel* was the nickname of the silver dollar.

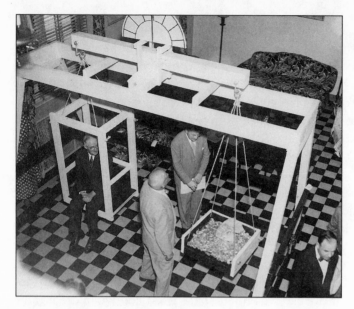

Charles F. Seabrook, president of Seabrook Farms, donated his weight in silver dollars to charity in 1950. *Courtesy of the Seabrook Educational and Cultural Center*

☞ *To Visit: Seabrook Educational and Cultural Center*

The Seabrook Educational and Cultural Center documents the history of the legendary agricultural operation and the people who made it happen. The center is located in the basement of the Upper Deerfield Township municipal building.

Seabrook Educational and Cultural Center
1325 Highway 77
Seabrook, NJ 08302
609-451-8393
Hours: Monday-Thursday, 10 A.M.-2 P.M.
Admission free; donations accepted.

Think of your favorite blueberry-laden dessert, then say thank you to the undisputed "Blueberry Queen," Elizabeth C. White (1871-1954). Without White, the oldest of four daughters of Quaker cranberry grower J. J. White, there might not be a marketable blueberry today. It was White who, in 1910, set out to turn the wild swamp huckleberry into the juicy, succulent blueberry to help supplement her father's thriving but seasonal cranberry business in the Pine Barrens.

White enlisted the services of local huckleberry pickers and deer hunters to find only the biggest huckleberries for use as parent material for controlled growth. Then she placed advertisements offering up to three dollars to anyone marking a bush that contained berries that would not drop through a hole ⅝ of an inch in diameter on a gauge she provided. She also appointed agents at strategic points within a 20-mile radius of her father's cranberry farm in Whitesbog, Burlington County, to create enthusiasm for her search.

White herself traveled many miles by horse and buggy and by foot over rough Pine Barren roads to seek out the marked huckleberry bushes. Ultimately, 100 bushes were found and named for their discoverers. Today, all cultivated blueberries are essentially descendants of eight bushes, seven found in New Jersey, and one found in New Hampshire by U.S. Department of Agriculture botanist Dr. Frederick Coville.

Coville's bush, the "Brooks," was crossed with White's "Sooy" bush and the Brooks-Sooy progeny were larger than either parent, creating blueberries ¾ of an inch in diameter. Yet another bush, discovered by Ruben Leek, also produced outstanding results. Usually White gave the bush the last name of its discoverer, but in this instance she couldn't call a blueberry bush the "Leek." Instead, she used Leek's first name, Rube, and added the first letter of his last name, to call this premiere bush the "Rubel."

Between 1912 and 1928, hundreds of thousands of blueberry plants were intentionally destroyed at Whitesbog. Only the superior plants were retained. The remaining plants were crossed with one another, and impeccable records were kept of the successes and failures. Commercial concerns were addressed, and varieties were created that would ripen at different times during the year to extend the blueberry's effective season. By 1928, there were acres of marketable blueberries, and the Whitesbog Blueberry Nursery joined J.J. White Company's cranberry business.

By the end of the 1920s, the wild huckleberry, with its large, crunchy seeds and hit-or-miss taste, had been transformed into a new, delicious fruit—the larger, darker, and sweeter blueberry with seeds so small they are barely discernible.

MARKETING AND PACKAGING INNOVATIONS

Elizabeth C. White's work with blueberries extended beyond the Pine Barrens and huckleberry swamps, reaching into the marketing and packaging of her products. She was the first to use cellophane on blueberry boxes, introducing the technique to the industry in 1916 after she located the product in Europe. Cellophane is, of course, still used today.

MASON JAR

In the 19th century, before the invention of refrigerators, food preservation presented a challenge for Americans. Winter diets were dreary and predictable in the first half of the 19th century, relying heavily on dried fruits and vegetables as the primary non-meat dishes. With the end of the growing season, fall marked the start of monotonous menus.

John Landis Mason, a native of Vineland, Cumberland County, helped change a nation's eating habits with the invention of the Mason jar in 1858. Since then, Mason's jars have been used, reused, and handed down

The Mason jar helped preserve food in an age before the invention of refrigerators. *Courtesy of the Courier-Post*

from one generation to the next, enabling families to preserve canned fruits, vegetables, and even fish and meat that taste fresher than those that are dried.

Expanding on the Theories of Others

Mason's invention built on the theories of Nicolas Appert, a French confectioner, who published his principles of food preservation through sterilization in 1810. Appert believed that heat would preserve vegetables, fruits, fish, and meats by deterring the inherent tendency of foods to spoil. Appert used glass containers in his experimentation because glass was the packaging material most resistant to air. French scientist Louis Pasteur discovered the scientific reasons for Appert's theories. Micro-organisms, responsible for food fermentation, could be destroyed with heat, and food could be kept in airtight glass.

Preserving the Harvest

Mason, born in Vineland in 1832, was the son of a farmer. His goal was to preserve the freshness of the fruits and vegetables that his father raised. After his 21st birthday, Mason moved to New York City to pursue his dream. The key for Mason was producing the threads atop a jar that would allow a metal cap to be screwed down, forming the all-important airtight seal.

In mid-November 1858, Mason received a patent for a glass jar with a threaded top. And on November 30, 1858, he received a patent for what he dubbed the "Improved Jar." In early 1859, Mason formed a partnership to produce the tops for the jars. The jars were ordered from glass blowers who had produced molds from Mason's patented specifications.

OTHER INVENTIONS

John Mason was a prolific inventor. His other inventions included a baby bottle, a folding life raft, a brush holder, and a die for a sheet metal cap.

Few Rewards for Mason

The first Mason jar was blown by Clayton Parker, a resident of Bridgeton, Cumberland County, working in a small glass factory owned by Samuel Crowley near Woodbury, Gloucester County. In 1861, the Civil War interrupted Mason's fledgling business, but the War Between the States helped spread the word about his invention.

After the war, Mason moved to New Brunswick, Middlesex County, where he married and started a family. He began working with the Consolidated Fruit Jar Company, which acquired the rights to his patents in 1873. The expiration of Mason's patents brought more companies into the jar-producing industry, and the firms that Mason was associated with were forced out of business. After the death of his wife in 1898, Mason moved back to New York City, where he fell on hard times financially and physically. He died at the age of 70 as a charity patient in a Manhattan hospital on February 26, 1902.

Mason's legacy has proved to be an enduring one, as sales of the Mason jar have exceeded the one billion mark in the more than 140 years since its invention.

AUTOMATION INCREASES PRODUCTION

A year after John Mason's death, the automatic bottlemaking machine was invented, increasing the production of the Mason jar and revolutionizing the glass container industry.

Government at Work

SUMMIT MEETING ON 24-HOUR NOTICE

"Location is everything" is an old real estate saying, and Glassboro, Gloucester County, proved it was just as true in international diplomacy in June 1967. The Gloucester County town's location—halfway between New York City and Washington, D.C.—led to its selection as

This historical marker was put up after President Lyndon Johnson and Soviet Premier Aleksei Kosygin met at Glassboro State College in June 1967.
Courtesy of the Courier-Post

the site for a Cold War summit meeting between President Lyndon Johnson and Soviet Premier Aleksei Kosygin from June 23 to 25, 1967.

The summit was not, in itself, a first. World leaders, after all, get together in what are usually well-planned and choreographed events all the time. The Glassboro summit was, however, the first time the leaders of what were then the world's two mightiest countries met in such a casual setting on less than 24 hours' notice. As a correspondent for the *Baltimore Sun* newspaper wrote in a June 24, 1967, article: "The talks in Holly Bush, a house on the campus of Glassboro State College [now Rowan University], were organized on what was undoubtedly the shortest notice ever given for world leaders."

All Eyes on Glassboro

The decision to hold the summit in Glassboro was one that caught everyone—from the 10,000 residents of the college town to members of the national media—by surprise. The summit and the subsequent attention it brought to Glassboro would be unprecedented. A report in the *Boston Globe* summed up the situation:

> Glassboro is considered to be jumping when its two centers of entertainment—a bowling alley and a movie house—fill up on a Saturday night. But today, for a few hours anyway, Glassboro will be the capital of the world.

Two events helped to set the stage for the summit—the Vietnam War and the Six-Day War in the Middle East that saw Israel defeat its Arab opponents. Tensions were on the rise between the United States and the Soviet Union. When Kosygin came to the United States for a meeting of the United Nations General Assembly in New York, suggestions were made that he and Johnson should meet.

A Geographic Compromise

When Kosygin would not come to Washington and Johnson declined to go to New York, New Jersey's governor, Richard Hughes, intervened and suggested New Jersey as a compromise meeting site for the two leaders. Governor Hughes proposed Glassboro as his top choice, later stating:

> I concentrated on finding a place that typified rural America, not too fancy and yet a locale having a dignified educational background which makes one think of youth and the great stake youth has in the peace of the world. The spot that met those requirements was Glassboro State College.

Once Johnson and Kosygin finally agreed to the meeting, little time was wasted in staging the event. The first announcement of the conference came at 6:30 P.M. on Thursday, June 22, 1967, with the leaders' first meeting set for 11 A.M. the following day. With memories of President Kennedy's assassination fresh in their minds, state and local police kept tight security in and around Glassboro. The borough's 16-man police force was augmented by more than 500 state troopers.

Around-the-Clock Preparations

Preparations went on around the clock for the summit. Air conditioning—a standard feature in most buildings today—had to be installed in the Holly Bush mansion where Johnson and Kosygin would meet. Telephones and teletype machines were set up in the college gymnasium to handle more than 1,000 members of the media.

Kosygin and Johnson met for five hours on June 23 and surprised the media and people waiting outside Holly Bush with an announcement that they would meet again on June 25. The leaders met for five more hours that Sunday. But no formal agreements were made. Still, the summit

Soviet Premier Aleksei Kosygin (left) and President Lyndon Johnson meet the press at Glassboro State College. *Courtesy of the* Courier-Post

should not be considered a failure. It marked the first time U.S. and Soviet leaders had met since President Kennedy and Nikita Khrushchev conferred in Vienna in 1961. After Glassboro, the leaders of the two superpowers would meet on a more frequent basis and never again would go as long as six years without a summit. Future summits would produce agreements on arms limitations and other important issues. In that sense, the Glassboro summit helped to ease the tensions of the Cold War.

TWO MORE PRESIDENTIAL VISITS

Glassboro would continue to be a favorite spot for presidents. President Johnson returned in 1968 to address the graduating class of Glassboro State College. And in 1986, President Reagan came to Glassboro High School to deliver the commencement address.

Aaron Burr and Alexander Hamilton enjoyed, to put it mildly, a stormy political relationship in the early years of the United States. Their rivalry climaxed in a deadly encounter between the two men in North Jersey in 1804, when Burr became the first (and hopefully the last) U.S. vice president to kill another man in a duel.

Hamilton and Burr were contemporaries who fought in the American Revolution. Hamilton was born in the British West Indies in January 1755. Burr was born 13 months later in Newark, Essex County. A captain in the provincial artillery, Hamilton became an aide-de-camp to General George Washington. Burr served on Washington's staff during the war but was transferred after antagonizing the general.

Alexander Hamilton, killed in a duel with political rival Aaron Burr in Weehawken in 1804, is pictured today on the $10 bill.

Political Bickering

Burr and Hamilton both entered the political arena after the new Constitution took effect in 1788. Hamilton became the first secretary of the Treasury under Washington, from 1789 to 1795, and while in office he established the Bank of the United States in 1791.

Burr became a state senator from New York in 1784 and was appointed attorney general in 1789. Two years later, he built a political coalition against Phillip Schuyler, Hamilton's father-in-law, and was elected to the U.S. Senate, becoming a political enemy of Hamilton. Burr lost his Senate re-election bid in 1797 but won the vice presidential nomination on a ticket with Thomas Jefferson in 1800. Under the procedures in place at the time, Jefferson and Burr each received 73 votes without designating who should be the president and who the vice president. The election was thrown into the House of Representatives where Hamilton, a key member of the Federalist Party, worked to ensure Jefferson's ascendancy to the presidency, further antagonizing Burr.

A few years later, in 1804, Burr was unsuccessful in his bid to become governor of New York, thanks to Hamilton's opposition, and George Clinton replaced Burr as the vice presidential candidate when Jefferson ran for re-election in 1804.

The Duo Duel

When Burr heard of Hamilton's comments questioning his character, he challenged Hamilton to a duel. The two men met in Weehawken, Hudson County, on July 11, 1804. Burr gravely wounded Hamilton, who died the next day at the age of 49.

By killing Hamilton, Burr also killed his own political career. After purchasing half a million acres of land in what is now northern Louisiana, Burr organized a colonizing expedition to the area. He believed that a war with Spain over the Mexican boundary was imminent. Burr was charged with scheming to form a separate nation and was put on trial for treason in 1807. He was acquitted since he had committed no overtly treasonous acts. Burr left the country under a cloud of mistrust and traveled in Europe. He returned to New York in 1812 and took up the practice of law. He died at the age of 80 in 1836.

NO MURDER TRIAL FOR BURR

Aaron Burr never stood trial for killing Alexander Hamilton, but Congress passed a bill, signed by President Thomas Jefferson, to outlaw dueling by federal officials. Hamilton is best known today as the face on the $10 bill.

PUBLIC SCHOOL TAKEOVER BY A STATE

New Jersey has always taken its commitment to education seriously, from its mandate that students receive a thorough and efficient education to its charter schools, creating an alternative to public schooling. In 1998, the state spent $10,189 per pupil, more than any other state and 68 percent higher than the national average.

When the Jersey City school district in Hudson County failed to adequately meet the educational needs of the city's children, the New Jersey Department of Education took unprecedented action by assuming day-to-day control of the district in 1989. It marked the first time any state had taken over a local school district. The New Jersey Board of Education appointed Elena J. Scambio to a three-year term as district superintendent.

In its bid to take control of Jersey City's schools, New Jersey had cited political intrusion in hiring practices involving nepotism, poor test scores, failure to provide a safe and clean environment for students, violations of bidding laws, failure to provide for handicapped children, and unautho-

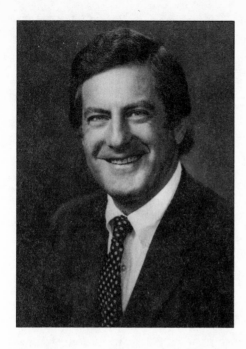

Dr. Saul Cooperman was the New Jersey Commissioner of Education when the state took over Jersey City schools.
Courtesy of the Courier-Post

rized use of state funds as among the reasons for the takeover. In some cases, students used textbooks more than 30 years old. A course on African American history, given in 1989, ended with the Nixon administration. At the time of the takeover, Jersey City was the second-largest school district in New Jersey, with 28,000 students.

A state report found that the local school board circumvented its purchase order process and bidding procedures, that two vendors received $3.5 million in excess of their authorization, and that public money was going to personal expenses, such as parking tickets. The report also found that hiring and firing decisions were made for political reasons and that turnover was rampant. "Positions are created, abolished and personnel transferred, demoted, promoted and hired with each change of municipal leadership," the report said.

Governor Thomas H. Kean said Jersey City students had been subjected to "educational child abuse. Now the community can put politics and patronage aside and get on with the business of learning." Commissioner of Education Saul Cooperman called the takeover "invasive surgery" that should be used only in rare instances.

In May 1988, after repeated monitoring of Jersey City schools, Cooperman issued an order demanding that Jersey City explain why it should not be taken over by the state. Administrative Law Judge Kenneth Springer heard testimony of witnesses for 104 days over an eight-month period in 1988 and 1989. He ruled on July 26, 1989, that abundant evidence existed that Jersey City children were being denied a decent education. "Children from impoverished backgrounds must not be condemned to poor schools," Springer wrote in his 75-page ruling. His decision cleared the way for the takeover. When Jersey City mayor Gerald McCann announced that he would not fight the state takeover, the battle for control of the school system finally ended.

Since the takeover by the state, conditions and test scores in Jersey City have improved somewhat, but not enough for the state to relinquish control. A spokesman for the New Jersey Department of Education said the state would not return control to local officials before 2000.

MORE TAKEOVERS

New Jersey's takeover of school districts did not stop with Jersey City. The state took control of public school districts in Paterson, Passaic County, in August 1991 and did the same in Newark, Essex County, in July 1995. Other states, including Kentucky, South Carolina, Texas, and New Mexico, have laws allowing state takeovers of failing school districts, according to the National Governors' Association.

WOMEN VOTE

More than 140 years before the ratification of the 19th Amendment provided women with a federal constitutional right to vote, New Jersey had blazed a trail—albeit a short-lived one—that had women heading to the polls in colonial America.

New Jersey's 1776 constitution, whether intentional or by oversight, did not specifically exclude women from the right to vote:

> All inhabitants of this colony of full age, who are worth fifty pounds proclamation money clear estate in the same, and have resided within the county in which they claim to vote twelve months immediately preceding the election shall be entitled to vote for representation in Council and Assembly and also for all other public officers that shall be elected by the people of the country at large.

Fifty pounds was a modest sum in 1776, and 95 percent of all white males met such a requirement. Married women could not meet this financial condition, though, since at that time all property automatically belonged to their husbands. Nevertheless, the impact of the Revolutionary War left many widows as landowners (it is estimated that approximately 5 percent of New Jersey land was then owned by women) who qualified under the new colony's constitution to cast their votes.

Right Reinforced in 1790 and 1797

It is unclear whether the language of the 1776 state constitution intentionally provided women the right to vote or was merely a oversight; after all, British troops were anchored off the New Jersey coast at the time the constitution was hastily drafted. Regardless of the original intent, however, a woman's right to vote was reinforced in 1790 when a subsequent election law explicitly allowed "he or she" to vote. This 1790 law, enacted by the legislature by a 33-4 vote, applied only to seven counties in the southern portion of the state where Quaker settlements and conservative, Federalist voters were concentrated—prompting historians to suggest that the law was motivated by politics rather than any notion of equality.

In 1797, a similar voting law was enacted, stating that "every voter shall openly and in full view deliver his or her ballot which shall be a single ticket containing the names of the person or persons for whom he or she votes...." This law's effect was extended statewide and, according to the *Trenton True American* newspaper, women accounted for 25 percent of the vote in that city in 1802. New Jersey women cast votes in the presidential election of 1800, helping to elect Thomas Jefferson.

Eventually, however, complaints began to arise over women's voting—contentions included that married women were casting votes and that some women were voting twice. The primary argument advanced by those in favor of state constitutional reform was that otherwise qualified women were not acting independently, but rather were casting their votes as directed by the men in their lives. William Griffith, a lawyer spearheading constitutional reform, called women's voting "perfectly disgusting" and said it amounted to voting by "persons who do not even pretend to any judgement on the subject."

Fraud at the Ballot Box

An election in 1802 in Hunterdon County was close enough to prompt charges that votes by married women, slaves, minors, and out-of-state residents affected the outcome. In 1807, a vote to decide the location of the Essex County Courthouse was held over three days, and evidence does indeed indicate a great deal of fraud, though not necessarily by either female or black voters. The 1807 election was manipulated—three times as many votes were cast in the city of Newark as had been cast the year before—and women voters were made to be scapegoats.

Later in 1807, John Condict of Essex County (who had nearly been defeated by women voters in his bid for election in Elizabethtown 10 years earlier) successfully introduced a law that restricted suffrage. His proposal simply stated that "from and after the passage of this act, no person shall vote in any state or county election for officers in the government of the United States, or of this state, unless such person be a free white male citizen of this state." While voting inconsistencies and irregularities were common in New Jersey elections at the time, women had become a political bull's eye and Condict's single sentence not only stripped women of their voting rights but also eliminated any property requirements for white males.

A RIGHT REGAINED

Women in New Jersey did not regain the right to vote for 113 years—until the enactment of the 19th Amendment to the U.S. Constitution on August 26, 1920. The amendment, approved by the U.S. House of Representatives and U.S. Senate on June 4, 1919, required ratification by 36 states. Illinois was the first to ratify on June 10, 1919, and New Jersey was the 29th to ratify on February 9, 1920. Tennessee was the 36th, ratifying the amendment on August 18, 1920.

NUCLEAR-POWERED PASSENGER-CARGO SHIP

The dropping of the first atomic bombs on Hiroshima and Nagasaki in August 1945 ushered the world into the nuclear age and brought about the end of World War II. And with the end of the war in Europe and the Pacific, the United States turned its attention to developing peacetime uses for nuclear energy.

First Lady Mamie Eisenhower wields a bottle of champagne as she christens the NS *Savannah* at New York Shipyard in Camden on July 21, 1959. With her are Louis E. Wolfson, chairman of the board of New York Shipbuilding Corporation, and Mrs. Henry B. Saylor, collector of customs at Savannah, Georgia.
Courtesy of the Courier-Post

President Dwight Eisenhower, who had served as the commander of allied forces in Europe during the war, proposed building the world's first nuclear-powered passenger-cargo ship during a speech on April 25, 1955. Four years after Eisenhower's proposal, the NS *Savannah* was launched into the Delaware River at Camden, Camden County, on July 21, 1959, fulfilling the president's dream.

The NS (short for "nuclear ship") *Savannah* was built at the New York Shipbuilding plant in Camden over a 14-month period between May 1958 and July 1959. Pat Nixon, wife of then-Vice President Richard Nixon, presided over the laying of the keel for the ship on May 22, 1958.

The NS *Savannah* was built at a cost of $40.25 million, with more than half of that money—$22.25 million—for developing and building the nuclear power plant aboard the ship. The NS *Savannah* used uranium oxide as its fissionable material for power, with pressurized water as the coolant. An auxiliary boiler and two diesel generators of 750-kilowatt capacity were included on the ship to provide power when the reactor was shut down. The ship was designed to travel 300,000 nautical miles without refueling. When construction was complete, the *Savannah* stood 595 feet long, or nearly the length of two football fields. Its sustained sea speed was 20.25 knots.

In signing the authorization for the NS *Savannah* in 1956, Eisenhower foresaw the ship as "the forerunner of atomic merchant and passenger fleets that will unite the nations of the world in peaceful trade." The ship failed to live up to that promise after its launching, but that failure was attributable to human squabbling rather than mechanical failure. Interunion arguments involving the ship's engineers and deck officers led to four strikes between 1960 and 1963. At one point, all 29 engineers serving on the ship were fired.

The NS *Savannah* approaches the Walt Whitman Bridge under auxiliary steam power as it heads to Yorktown, Virginia, on January 31, 1962. *Courtesy of the Courier-Post*

Proof of Nuclear's Potential

When it was in operation, the NS *Savannah* lived up to its billing. In one year of commercial operation, it made seven voyages to European and Mediterranean ports and logged 72,000 miles while consuming just 26 pounds of uranium fuel. The ship also was credited with furthering nuclear ship design technology and educating the shipping world about the feasibility of nuclear power.

In the end, the ship's survival came down to a matter of money. It was removed from service in August 1967 because of high operating costs. "Continued operation was not feasible against the overall financial needs of the country," a U.S. Maritime Administration spokesman said at the time. Officials of the Maritime Administration claimed it cost the government more than $3 million per year to keep the ship running—a figure that "significantly exceeded" revenues. The expenses involved the special maintenance, shore support, and crew training required for a nuclear vessel.

NEW SHIP, OLD NAME

The NS *Savannah* was named for another historic ship. The SS *Savannah* sailed on May 22, 1819, and became the first steam vessel to cross the Atlantic Ocean. The laying of the keel for the NS *Savannah* took place 139 years to the day the SS *Savannah* began its voyage to Europe.

That's Entertainment!

THE FIRST MUSIC ALBUM RECORDED IN AN AUTOMOBILE

As a subject matter for songs and a place to hear music, cars and rock 'n' roll go together like guitars and amplifiers. Musicians from Chuck Berry to the Beach Boys to Bruce Springsteen have explored that musical-automotive link.

Ben Vaughn took it to the extreme by recording his 1996 album, *Rambler '65* (Rhino), in his car of the same name while it was parked in the driveway of his Collingswood, Camden County, home. It was a case of American music meeting American Motors. "Rock 'n' roll and cars—

This is the cover of *Rambler '65*, the compact disc that Ben Vaughn recorded in his automobile.
Courtesy of Rhino Records

Ben Vaughn turned the back seat of his 1965 Rambler into a recording studio.
Photo by Greg Allen, courtesy of Rhino Records

to me you can't separate them," said Vaughn. "Rock 'n' roll never sounds better than it does on a car radio. Why not record it in a car?"

Necessity and Curiosity

The idea for recording the album in his car grew out of economic necessity and musical curiosity. "At the time, I had no record deal and no advance [money] for recording," said Vaughn, who was looking for a way to keep costs down. In addition, he wondered what kind of sound he could get while making music in a car. After recording a song, many musicians will listen to it on a car's sound system to see how it sounds. Vaughn tested the sound in his Rambler by recording his guitar. He liked what he heard, and the idea for recording an album in his car was born. (He also owns a 1964 Rambler but found his 1965 sounded better after recording in both vehicles.) "I knew I had to do it because I knew if I didn't I was going to get scooped," he said with a chuckle. "U2 would be recording in their limousine."

Vaughn set up the recording equipment in his front seat and played bass, guitar, and drum machines in the back seat with his amplifier in the trunk. He did all the vocals and played all the instruments on the album except for a sitar solo by Mike Vogelmann.

The automobile as recording studio presented some problems. Bees got into the car during the recording process. "It's hard to get away from bees when you've got headphones on and are strapped into a car with a bass guitar in your hand, playing loud music," Vaughn said. "At one point a bee went after me, so I lunged out of the car and took half the equipment with me because I was attached to it." Vaughn also found the recording process forced him to deliver his best performances on the first take. "Everything was a good take, mainly because of the claustrophobia. I just had to get the hell out of there."

HOLLYWOOD CONNECTIONS

Ben Vaughn is probably best known as the music composer for the NBC television shows *Third Rock from the Sun* and *Men Behaving Badly*. He is known for offbeat recording projects. *Mono U.S.A.* is a 1994 album of oldies recorded in monaural sound in his Collingswood home studio for $140. He also put together a tribute album built around the songs of the late Sonny Bono called—what else?—*Bonograph*.

The resulting album was devoid of the studio gloss found on modern recordings but retained a low-fi charm on such songs as "Seven Days Without Love" and "Song for You." Vaughn even recorded the sound of an airplane passing over his car as the introduction for the song "The Only

Way to Fly." "It's ragged but right," he said, borrowing from a line by country singer George Jones. Vaughn also succeeded in keeping his costs down. *Rambler '65* cost only $48 to make.

FIRST ROCK 'N' ROLL STAR

Bill Haley was blind in his left eye and near-sighted in his right one, but the former Salem County resident pursued a musical vision that would make him the first rock 'n' roll superstar.

It was during an 18-month engagement in the early 1950s at the Twin Bar at Broadway and Market Street in Gloucester City, Camden County, that Haley successfully blended country and western, rhythm and blues, and other musical styles to come up with rock 'n' roll. "Bill described it as the

Bill Haley and his Comets enjoyed international success in the 1950s. In the later years of his career, Haley performed his hit "Rock Around the Clock" at many rock 'n' roll oldies shows.
Courtesy of the Courier-Post

birthplace of rock 'n' roll, a place where he could experiment with the crowd," said John von Hoelle, co-author of *Sound and Glory*, a 1990 biography of the singer written with Haley's oldest son, Jack.

"Cowboy Jive"

Haley was an unlikely candidate to be a rock 'n' roll star. He was a country musician, songwriter, and disc jockey—on such stations as WSNJ-AM in Bridgeton—whose early inspirations were Hank Williams and cowboy singing star Gene Autry. Haley had been a struggling country singer since the mid-1940s but noticed audience approval when he added elements of rhythm and blues and its amplified beat to his music.

At the Twin Bar, Haley and his backing band, the Saddlemen, would start out playing country music but would switch gears around 10 P.M. Haley, von Hoelle writes, would tell the crowd: "All you hillbillies out there gotta go home now, because we're gonna play a little something we call cowboy jive. And we're the only band crazy enough to play it. So all you hillbillies cut loose and let the cool cats in, cause we're gonna rock this joint tonight."

TOP-SELLING 45 RPM RECORD OF ALL TIME

"Rock Around the Clock" was used as the opening theme on early episodes of the TV series *Happy Days* and was reissued as a single in 1974. It became Bill Haley's 13th and final Top 40 hit. He recorded the first 12 Top 40 hits between 1954 and 1958. "Rock Around the Clock" is recognized by the *Guinness Book of World Records* as the top-selling 45 rpm record of all time, with unaudited sales of more than 25 million copies worldwide. Haley was inducted into the Rock and Roll Hall of Fame in Cleveland, Ohio, in January 1987.

"Rock the Joint," the song the band launched into, would be a turning point in Haley's career. Released as a single in the spring of 1952, it was his most successful record to date, selling 75,000 copies, and it turned Haley's career away from country and toward rock 'n' roll. The Saddlemen, Haley's backing band, would become the Comets. The song's influence went beyond its sales. Haley liked the guitar solo so much that he repeated it note for note on "Rock Around the Clock."

Haley's commercial and artistic breakthrough came with the recording of "Rock Around the Clock" in April 1954. Although it was not a hit initially, it became a No. 1 single after it was used in the 1955 movie *Blackboard Jungle*. It became Haley's signature song.

While Haley's success would later be overshadowed by such stars as Elvis Presley, Chuck Berry, and Buddy Holly, he established a musical sound and direction for others to follow. In later years, however, Haley's role in the development of rock 'n' roll was downplayed, a fact that would bother him until his death in February 1981 at the age of 55. "The story has gotten pretty crowded as to who was the father of rock 'n' roll," he said in a 1970s interview. "I haven't done much in life except that, and I'd like to get credit for it."

DRIVE-IN MOVIE THEATER

As the story goes, Richard Hollingshead's mother was a large woman. So large, in fact, that she couldn't fit comfortably into the seats used in the single-screen, downtown movie theaters so popular in the 1930s. She apparently mentioned in passing that it would be wonderful if she could watch a movie from the plush comfort of her automobile. Like any good son, Richard acted on his mother's comment and launched the drive-in movie industry.

In June 1933, Hollingshead used a 16-millimeter film projector, the white wall of his automotive parts machine shop, and its parking lot on what is now Admiral Wilson Boulevard (formerly Bridge Boulevard), near the

Drive-ins caught on in popularity in New Jersey and the rest of the country after the first one opened in 1933 in Camden County. This drive-in collected a defense tax on its admission to help the military during World War II.
Courtesy of the Courier-Post

border of Camden and Pennsauken, to effectively create the world's first drive-in movie theater. (One building is still standing; it is part of what is now Zinman Furs.)

Hollingshead formed Park-In Theatres Inc. to show family-oriented movies on the back wall of the machine shop, charging one dollar per family or 75 cents for two people. The term "drive-in" came later when the industry reached its popularity peak in the 1950s, with nearly 4,000 theaters across the country. At its birth, Hollingshead's creation was known as the automobile movie theater.

Traditional movie theater operators immediately recognized the threat of drive-in movies and made it difficult for drive-ins to get first-run features in a timely manner. The movies shown were often edited for length and the earliest sound systems were merely outside loudspeakers shared by all patrons. Ultimately, the loudspeakers were replaced by single speakers for each car; today's remaining drive-ins (only about 800 survive) can pipe stereo sound to their guests through an automobile's FM radio channels.

Hollingshead's first automobile movie theater was more than just a solution to a personal seating problem. This entrepreneur actually obtained a patent on the ramp parking system that allowed unobstructed views for all cars. When that patent was overturned in 1949, drive-in movie theaters hit their stride and reached the height of their popularity in the late 1950s, often using leased land in wide open rural areas. But as residents migrated from cities to suburbs, that same land often became prime residential or retail building property and thus increased in value to the point that it was economically illogical for use as a drive-in theater.

FIRST MARTIAN ATTACK

On Mischief Night, October 30, 1938, Mars launched its first attack on our planet, landing its warship in Grover's Mill (now West Windsor Township) near Princeton, Mercer County, and then spraying New Jersey and New York City with poisonous gases.

Orson Welles spoofed his 1938 "War of the Worlds" broadcast during an appearance on *Rowan and Martin's Laugh-In* that was originally broadcast on NBC television on October 26, 1970. *Courtesy of the* Courier-Post

Orson Welles revolutionized the motion picture industry with his 1938 film *Citizen Kane*.
Courtesy of the Courier-Post

The interplanetary conflict led to mass destruction, a monumental death count (as high as 7,000), and incredible shock and hysteria throughout the country as events were reported live between 8:15 and 9:30 P.M. on WABC Radio and the Columbia Broadcasting System's coast-to-coast network.

Some 60 years later, the shock and hysteria are known to be real, but the "news" broadcast is recognized as one of radio's great hoaxes—it was merely a radio adaptation of H. G. Wells' 1896 novel, *The War of the Worlds*, directed by future movie giant Orson Welles, then just 23 years old.

Unexpected Reaction?

Whether the radio play was actually intended to create such widespread panic remains in dispute. After all, the *New York Times* noted in accounts after the uproar that newspaper listings announced the "Mercury Theatre" performance for the day as "Play: H. G. Wells' War of the Worlds" and disclaimers that the event was fiction were played before, during, and after the broadcast.

On the other hand, the play was broadcast at the same time as the most popular radio program of the day, *The Bergen-McCarthy Hour*. It was widely known that part way through *The Bergen-McCarthy Hour* an appearance by a guest artist would have listeners changing their radio dial. This channel surfing would lead many listeners to the "Mercury Theatre" at a time after the initial disclaimer was announced on the air.

For authenticity, the news simulation broke into an otherwise ordinary dance program and utilized convincing news-reporting techniques. The English "attack" locations in H. G. Wells' novel were changed to places in New Jersey. Orson Welles and the actors capably portrayed federal, state, and municipal officials, with one even impersonating Franklin Roosevelt (as "Secretary of the Interior") to provide emergency instructions.

Today, a Laughing Matter

Intended or not, the results of the broadcast were, upon reflection six decades later, almost comical:

- In Newark, more than 20 families rushed to the streets with wet handkerchiefs and towels over their faces to avoid the poisonous gas, causing more chaos with a traffic jam that spread the "news" of the impending doom.
- The *New York Times* received 875 calls. One man from Dayton, Ohio, merely asked, "What time will it be the end of the world?"
- Thirty people rushed into a police station in New York City, reporting their bags were packed and they were ready for instructions on evacuation.

- Jersey City police fielded dozens of calls, one asking whether the department could provide gas masks; East Orange police received more than 200 calls.
- At St. Michael's Hospital in Newark, 15 men and women were treated for shock and hysteria; a Pittsburgh man stopped his wife from taking poison as she screamed, "I'd rather die this way than like that."
- The radio play became so real that there were first-hand reports of people "seeing" the invasion and the flames from the attack; families in Boston sat on their rooftops, claiming that they were able to see the glow of a burning New York City.
- Panic reached as far as the West Coast, and in Indiana a woman burst into a church hollering: "New York is destroyed; it's the end of the world. You might as well go home to die. I just heard it on the radio." Church services were immediately ended.
- Geologists at Princeton University received news of the "event" and went to nearby Dutch Neck to search for the reported meteor (which was later determined in the play to be a cylinder carrying armed Martians). All they found at the site were others looking for the same thing.

After order was restored, many listeners were outraged by the broadcast. The Columbia Broadcasting System issued an explanation and expressed regret at the reaction to the broadcast. Orson Welles was astounded at the results. He said he had hesitated presenting the radio play because he thought people might be bored by a story so improbable!

ROCK STAR SIMULTANEOUSLY ON *TIME* AND *NEWSWEEK* COVERS

As 1975 dawned, Bruce Springsteen's musical career was at a crossroads. The New Jersey native was laboring over the recording of his third album, unable to capture the energy of his live performances that led music critic Jon Landau to write, "I have seen rock 'n' roll's future and its name is Bruce Springsteen."

By the end of that year, Springsteen would be on the road to stardom, with the September release of his third album, *Born to Run;* its title track would be his first hit single. The publicity and critical praise for the album would land Springsteen on the covers of *Time* and *Newsweek,* for both of their October 27, 1975, issues, making him the first rock musician to appear on the cover of both newsmagazines simultaneously—a feat that had eluded even such earlier superstars as Elvis Presley and the Beatles.

Nine years after appearing on the covers of *Time* and *Newsweek* magazines in the same week, Bruce Springsteen became an international superstar with the release of his *Born in the USA* album in 1984. *Courtesy of the* Courier-Post

Musical Beginnings

Born in Freehold, Monmouth County, the 26-year-old Springsteen would seem to have been an unlikely cover subject. His first two albums, *Greetings from Asbury Park, N.J.* and *The Wild, the Innocent and the E Street Shuffle*, were both released in 1973 to a favorable reception by critics but achieved only lukewarm sales. Neither album cracked *Billboard* magazine's list of the top 50 best-selling albums in the country.

Nevertheless, Springsteen built a fan base in the Northeast in the early 1970s because of his concerts, which could last three or four hours each.

"Born to Run" had been released to selected radio stations in 1974 and had left fans wanting more, since it was commercially unavailable at the time.

Springsteen enlisted Landau to serve as co-producer of *Born to Run* in 1975, to help him break his creative logjam. The album started taking shape during the spring and summer of that year. *Time* and *Newsweek* began to take an interest in the Springsteen phenomenon and their cover stories coincided the last week of October. *Time* heralded Springsteen as "Rock's Newest Sensation," while *Newsweek* headlined its cover with the phrase "The Making of a Rock Star." They gave an important boost to Springsteen's career in an era before cable television, MTV, and the Internet.

A TRIBUTE TO FRANK SINATRA

Twenty-three years after Springsteen's feat, another New Jersey native and musician, Frank Sinatra, raised in Hoboken, would appear on the covers of *Time* and *Newsweek* for both May 25, 1998, editions. The newsmagazines paid tribute to the legendary singer soon after his death at age 82.

Shore Things

THE FIRST INDOOR COLLEGE FOOTBALL BOWL GAME

Convention Hall in Atlantic City, Atlantic County, gained national fame as the venue for the annual Miss America Pageant, but it has also grabbed a national spotlight in the field of sports. In fact, it served as the site of the first indoor college football bowl game when it hosted the sixth annual Liberty Bowl in December 1964.

The December 1963 Liberty Bowl had been played in Memorial Stadium in Philadelphia. Temperatures in the low 20s along with winds that reached 17 miles per hour had frozen the wallets of most college

The first indoor college football bowl game, the Liberty Bowl, was played in Atlantic City's Convention Hall in 1964.
Courtesy of the Atlantic City Historical Museum

football fans. Only 8,309 people turned out to watch Mississippi defeat North Carolina, 16-12. Liberty Bowl president Bud Dudley had a bigger number on his mind—93,691. That was how many seats were vacant in cavernous Memorial Stadium.

Anxious to attract more fans, Dudley wanted to move the game to a location in the mid-Atlantic region that was immune to winter's chill. If he could capture the media's attention, that would be a bonus. He chose Convention Hall for the 1964 game, which matched Utah and West Virginia. This Liberty Bowl was not the first college football game played indoors. Ironically, Convention Hall had attained that first in 1930 when Lafayette played Washington and Jefferson.

By landing the Liberty Bowl, Atlantic City wound up hosting the first indoor college bowl game four months before the Astrodome in Houston even opened. When Utah and West Virginia met, the temperature was a chilly 31°F outside, a comfortable 60°F inside. "It was the only bowl I ever promoted where a coach complained it was a bit too warm," Dudley quipped.

No Shivering in the Stands

As Philadelphia *Evening Bulletin* sports columnist Sandy Grady observed, it was "a new kind of Liberty Bowl—no frostbite, no hip flasks, no icy ear-

ABOUT CONVENTION HALL

Until the Houston Astrodome opened in 1965, Convention Hall (which opened in May 1929) was the largest room without pillars in the United States. The football field for the bowl games fit—well, almost. The end zone was actually shortened by two yards because of the intimidating presence of Convention Hall's mammoth stage. At 137 feet, the roof is high enough to allow a helicopter to touch down inside the building.

Atlantic City's Convention Hall was the site of the world's first indoor helicopter flight in November 1970. *Courtesy of the* Courier-Post

lobes." Indoor football, dubbed "parlorball" by the columnist, avoided the elements—including the element of suspense—as Utah, led by future Pittsburgh Steelers star Roy Jefferson, trounced West Virginia, 32-6.

The game was a qualified success. Players and coaches for both teams praised the indoor field—real sod, not artificial turf, was used. Playing the game indoors allowed ABC television, which broadcast the game to a national audience, to try out unique camera angles. The network placed a camera in the rafters of Convention Hall, 13 floors above the ground, to provide an aerial view of the plays unfolding. Jack Gould, writing for the *New York Times*, was impressed: "The perspective was little short of astonishing. The legendary seat on the 50-yard line has lost its status as the best place to watch a game."

Ticket sales, though, were a bit disappointing. Only 6,059 out of a possible 12,000 seats were sold at $10 a seat. A capacity of 50 percent, however, was still markedly better than the minuscule 8 percent for the previous year in Philadelphia. Thanks to $95,000 in broadcast fees paid by ABC, Dudley made a profit of $5,000, which was donated to local charities.

The Liberty Bowl moved to Memphis in 1965 and has been played there ever since. Convention Hall, meanwhile, would host the Boardwalk Bowl (the NCAA Division II regional championship game) from 1968 to 1973 and the Knute Rockne Bowl (the NCAA Division III regional championship game) from 1970 to 1972. The last college football game played at Convention Hall was on November 30, 1984, between Temple and the University of Toledo.

MISS AMERICA PAGEANT

Sixteen-year-old Margaret Gorman stood just an inch over five feet tall, weighed in at 108 pounds, and the tape measured her vital statistics at a less-than-curvaceous 30-25-32—a long stroll on the Boardwalk from today's physical beauty standards. But *there she was* in Atlantic City, Atlantic County, in September 1921, accepting the crown as the winner of the first Miss America Pageant.

That first pageant was intended only to be a small part of the multi-faceted "Fall Frolic," which local business owners had concocted a year earlier to help Atlantic City extend its tourism season beyond the traditional end-of-summer Labor Day weekend. In addition to the Miss America beauty pageant, there were numerous events on the Boardwalk and a comic bathing suit contest on the sand between Garden and Steel Piers.

Newspapers Select Local Winners

In order to attract contestants for the first beauty pageant, local organizers selected newspapers along the East Coast (as far west as Pittsburgh and as far south as Washington, D.C.) and invited the papers to solicit and print photos of potential competitors. (Participating newspapers could use their involvement in choosing contestants for the pageant as a gimmick to increase their circulation.) The newspapers then selected a winner to represent them in the pageant and paid for the entrant's

Tiny Margaret Gorman, representing Washington, D.C., was crowned the first Miss America in 1921 in Atlantic City. *Courtesy of Vicki Gold Levi collection*

wardrobe. Atlantic City footed the bill for transportation and a week-long stay at the resort.

Margaret Gorman, the daughter of the executive clerk to the U.S. secretary of agriculture, and six other "beauty maids" were selected by the newspapers to compete in the non-professional beauty competition; no actresses, motion picture stars, or professional swimmers were permitted to enter this field. Tiny Margaret, who represented Washington, D.C., won the "beauty urn"; Miss Camden, Kathryn Gearon, finished as first runner-up.

As winner among the "Civic Beauties," Miss Gorman was then pitted in a sort of playoff against the winner of the professional competition, Virginia Lee from New York City. The five judges, including artist Howard Chandler Christy and actor John Drew, awarded blond-haired, blue-eyed

Margaret the grand trophy, a golden statue of a mermaid, three feet long and 10 inches high. Its value was placed at $1,500, but it was actually worth about $50.

"Happy? Why, I am the happiest girl in the wide world, and I have every reason to think so," Miss Gorman told the *Atlantic City Press* after the event. "No, I have not received any invitation to enter the screen field. I don't know just what I would do if such an offer came to me." No such offer came; she returned to high school with little fanfare.

There She Is...Miss Inter-City Beauty Maid

While the "Miss America" title had been coined as early as 1921 by pageant publicist Herb Test of the *Atlantic City Press*, it was seldom used until later years. Margaret Gorman was more commonly referred to as the "Inter-City Beauty Maid Contest" winner.

The Miss America Pageant expanded from seven entrants in the non-professional division in 1921 to 57 girls in 1922, this time coming from as far away as Los Angeles, Seattle, and San Francisco. Miss Columbus, Ohio, auburn-haired Mary Katherine Campbell, then age 15 (though she told organizers she was 16, the minimum age), was the winner in 1922. At 5-foot-7 and 140 pounds, she was six inches taller and nearly 30 pounds heavier than Margaret Gorman; her measurements—35-26-36—essentially set the tone for the judging of hour-glass figures in future pageants.

Miss Campbell became the pageant's only repeat winner in 1923, when she won out over 75 contestants. Margaret Gorman also competed in 1922 and 1923; Mary Katherine Campbell's bid for three consecutive crowns was thwarted in 1924 when Miss Philadelphia, Ruth Malcolmson, won out over the pageant's largest field ever—83 entrants.

SALT WATER TAFFY

A visit to the New Jersey Boardwalk would not be complete without a sampling of salt water taffy. Call it one of the great marketing efforts of the 20th century.

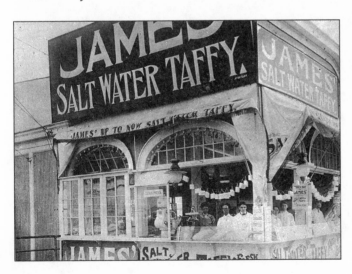

James' Salt Water Taffy was one of the first companies to produce the candy treat on Atlantic City's Boardwalk in the late 1800s. *Courtesy of James Candy Co.*

Taffy by itself is by no means a New Jersey first or unique to the state. *Salt water* taffy, on the other hand, is a New Jersey Boardwalk invention, complete with reams of folklore and multiple claims of legendary marketing genius.

First, there's the story—undocumented, of course, but "witnessed" by numbers that grow greater as time passes—of the confectioner making taffy on the Boardwalk in Atlantic City, Atlantic County, in the 1870s, who left his sweets to cool on the beach. A wave washed over the candy, dousing it with salt water. The astute businessman, not anxious to lose his day's work, successfully sold the candy as salt water taffy—and an industry was born.

Second, there's the contention that any number of sharp shop owners deftly utilized the phrase "salt water" to describe their boxed taffy (and other

Fralinger's postcards remind Atlantic City visitors that no one leaves the Boardwalk without a box of salt water taffy.
Courtesy of James Candy Co.

foods) to capitalize on the perceived medicinal value of the ocean's salt water. Even today, the myth surrounding the healing powers of salt water lives on.

Plenty of Sugar, a Pinch of Salt

The truth of the matter is that ocean water, medicinal or not, has no place among the ingredients of salt water taffy. A pinch of salt is utilized, water is an ingredient—but the closest *salt water* gets to the process is a beachgoer's wet bathing suit. Sugar, of course, is the primary ingredient.

Much of the early success of salt water taffy can actually be attributed to the packaging of the candy. In the late 1800s, the two forefathers of salt water taffy, competitors Enoch James and Joseph Fralinger, each boxed their candies in tin containers adorned with scenes of Atlantic City that became keepsakes after the candy was eaten.

TODAY'S TAFFY

Fralinger's and James' remain the top sellers of salt water taffy to this day. The two companies have merged, but their candy is sold under separate labels. Close to 20 flavors are now sold, and the old standbys, chocolate and vanilla, remain the top sellers. During World War II, even with sugar shortages, a one-pound box of assorted taffy cost about 35 cents. Today, a one-pound box sells for about five dollars.

THE BOARDWALK

Everybody loves New Jersey's beaches. Sun, ocean waves, and salt water taffy. Perfect together. But, oh, the sand!

In 1870, Alexander Boardman and Jacob Keim knew all too well about the sand. Boardman owned a small Atlantic City hotel and was a conduc-

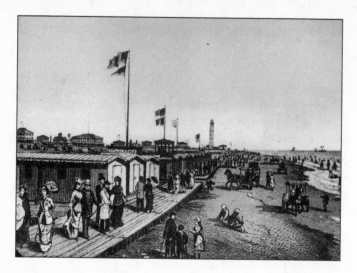

A rendering of Atlantic City's Boardwalk, the world's first, circa 1870. *Courtesy of Vicki Gold Levi collection*

tor on the Camden & Atlantic Railroad. Keim was another hotel owner. Their hotel lobbies and lobby furniture were being overcome by the unsightly and irritating sand from the beach. And the railcars needed constant sweeping as passengers boarded with sandy feet and sandy suits.

Boardman had a solution. He wanted to build a wooden walkway along the upper edge of the beach that would help reduce the amount of sand tracked into the hotels and railcars. The walkway would also give vacationers somewhere to walk with a view of the ocean but without the perils of wet or hot sand (splinters are another story). Keim heard of the idea and together they presented this "sans sand" solution to other hotel operators and eventually to the city council. Hotel operators unanimously supported the concept and there was apparently a growing wave of support from vacationers aware of the idea, too. The proposal was approved without opposition by the council, and in June 1870, the world's first "Boardwalk" was dedicated in Atlantic City, Atlantic County.

An early postcard (circa 1904) reflects the beach attire of the period, as well as the progress of the Atlantic City Boardwalk since its introduction in the 1870s. *Courtesy of the Atlantic City Historical Museum*

"Keimwalk" Just Didn't Sound Right

While Alexander Boardman was the driving force behind the walkway, the new contraption was not named after him—the name was purely coincidental. And that first boardwalk in 1870 was a far cry from the commercial monsters that today are a staple of New Jersey shore resorts. The first boardwalk, for example, was built in 12-foot sections and was just 18 inches above the sand. It was also portable; the 12-foot sections were disassembled at the end of each vacation season and stored until the following summer.

The new boardwalk was an instant hit with residents and vacationers—even without T-shirt shops, pork roll, cotton candy, salt water taffy, amusements, and piers. Initially, no buildings were permitted to be built within 30 feet of it.

☞ *To Visit: Atlantic City Historical Museum*

The Atlantic City Historical Museum preserves the diverse folklore of the unique seaside resort in a presentation that includes a miniature beach and Boardwalk overlooking a spectacular view of the real thing. Revolving exhibitions in the Al Gold Photography Gallery offer picturesque images of historic interest.

Atlantic City Historical Museum
Garden Pier
New Jersey Avenue at the Boardwalk
Atlantic City, NJ 08401
609-347-5839
Hours: Daily, 10 A.M.-4 P.M.
Closed major holidays.
Admission free.

FIRST SEASHORE RESORT

When Postmaster Ellis Hughes of Cape May, Cape May County, placed a wordy advertisement in the *Philadelphia Daily Aurora* newspaper in June 1801, soliciting visitors for "sea bathing" in his community, he unknowingly solidified Cape May's claim as the nation's first seashore resort.

Depending on just how "resort" is defined, though, Long Branch in Monmouth County and Newport, Rhode Island, can both make legitimate

When the Virginia Hotel in Cape May was renovated, the owners added air conditioning. Some of the bathrooms that were added can be seen overhanging the side of the building. *Courtesy of the Courier-Post*

The Inn of Cape May was once the town's largest building.
Courtesy of the Courier-Post

arguments that they were the first seashore resort. After all, those towns (like Cape May and probably many other seaside communities) had seashores and visitors well before 1801. But when Postmaster Hughes placed his advertisement, Cape May at the very least became the first community to promote its oceanside location as a summer resort.

The advertisement, in part, read: "The subscriber has prepared himself for entertaining company who use sea bathing, and he is accommodated with extensive house room, with fish, oysters and crabs and good liquors—Care will be taken of gentlemen's Horses." And while the solicitation might seem mundane in today's era of monstrous multi-media marketing campaigns, Postmaster Hughes' advertisement impressed many of his contemporaries, enough anyway to help start Cape May on the path to becoming the world's premier summer resort during most of the 1800s.

On the Way to Cape May

The earliest visitors to Cape May rode stagecoaches from Cooper's Ferry (now Camden), leaving at 4 A.M. and not arriving until after midnight. Later, coach trips directly from Philadelphia to Cape May took two days

Vacationers relax on the porch of the Chalfonte Hotel in Cape May.
Courtesy of the Courier-Post

since part of a day was spent resting horses. Eventually, sailing vessels carried passengers there, making the trip much more comfortable. The first regular steamboat service from Philadelphia began in 1819. Visitors stayed in farmhouses, taverns, or boarding houses along the coast until the 1830s, when the first of what would be many large hotels were built.

Early ocean use was far from the boogie boarding and wave riding we see today. In fact, Cape May's "sea bathing" consisted of wading in the water and jumping joyously up and down in the surf. Mixed bathing was taboo for the first half of the 19th century; different colored flags along the beach marked separate bathing times for men and women.

Long Branch, a Strong Contender

Long Branch's development as a resort ran nearly parallel to that of Cape May. Both resorts attracted rich socialites from Philadelphia, New York, and Baltimore, and at least 10 different presidents summered in either Cape May or Long Branch (Lincoln, Pierce, Hayes, Grant, Buchanan,

Harrison, Garfield, Wilson, McKinley, and Arthur). Although blue laws prevailed in the early 1800s, both resorts ultimately allowed a shift toward dancing, drinking, and legalized gambling to define their high-profile role during the second half of the 19th century. By 1900, both had lost their luster among the rich and famous, who were by then making Newport, Rhode Island, the summer resort of choice. Today, both Cape May and Long Branch are firmly entrenched among the state's finest family resorts.

ALL EYES ON LONG BRANCH

Long Branch captured the world's attention in 1881 when President James A. Garfield was shot in Washington, D.C., on July 2. The president underwent two operations at the White House to remove two bullets and was eventually transported to Long Branch on September 2, 1881, at his doctors' suggestion that he be moved to escape the unusually high temperatures in Washington at the time. On September 11, it was determined that blood poisoning had affected President Garfield's right lung. Despite an attempt at leeching, Garfield died in Long Branch on September 18, 1881, becoming the second U.S. president to succumb to an assassin's attack.

COME WITH ME, INTO THE SEA

Even if Long Branch must take a back seat to Cape May on the seashore resort timeline, the Monmouth County resort can rightfully make a claim for a first of its own. While mixed-gender sea bathing was initially frowned upon, it became commonplace in the second half of the 19th century. In fact, by the 1880s, no fashionable belle would bathe without a male escort. This tradition led to the introduction of the first American gigolos in Long Branch—not as dancing partners but as sea-bathing companions!

PICTURE POSTCARD

Today, mailing souvenir picture postcards is a mandatory part of any vacation. Travelers feel a sense of obligation to remind their families or perhaps their co-workers back at the office that they are having a good time, that "we wish you were here," and that their dream vacation destination is indeed as pretty as the picture on the postcard.

But in 1895, there was no such thing as a souvenir postcard—at least not in the United States. That year, the wife of Atlantic City, Atlantic County, printer Carl M. Voelker returned to her childhood home on the Rhine River in Germany. She brought back to New Jersey (apparently she did not mail them) an assortment of picture cards then on sale in Germany.

The enterprising Mr. Voelker figured he would parlay his printing business and his location in a booming seashore resort town into a new revenue stream. He printed 10,000 color postcards with the intention of selling them to hotels and businesses in Atlantic City for use as advertising. However, sales to businesses were disappointing and Voelker was left holding most of the postcards; he had nothing but red ink on his hands.

With the "new" Steel Pier in the background, picture postcards of resorts made their debut in Atlantic City. This card is one of the earliest, produced about 1898.
Courtesy of the Atlantic City Historical Museum

As a result, he began to sell the remaining cards to vacationers as souvenirs at bargain prices. Within a few seasons, the picture postcard—it required half the postage and a lot less words to fill than a letter—was as much a part of Atlantic City as sun and salt water. Voelker's postcards actually changed the way the local post office did business. By 1906, the Atlantic City Post Office handled 1.5 million postcards in the month of August alone. The one-cent stamp needed for postcards outsold the traditional two-cent business stamp by a five-to-one margin in Atlantic City.

THE ROLLING CHAIR

Where better to enjoy salt water taffy and write a picture postcard than from the comfort of a rolling chair on the Boardwalk? You could get four New Jersey firsts rolled into one leisurely ride.

The rolling chair so prominent on boardwalks along the East Coast during the late 1800s and early 1900s made its American debut on the Atlantic City boards in 1884, when entrepreneur M. D. Shill, an Atlantic City hardware dealer, set up a stall to rent the rolling chairs. The chairs had first been

The rolling chair became a featured item on picture postcards. Both the chair and the cards themselves are New Jersey firsts. This card is from the early 1900s. *Courtesy of the Atlantic City Historical Museum*

used eight years earlier at the Philadelphia Centennial Exhibition to help move visitors around the expansive grounds.

Shill offered the chairs complete with "pushers"—an innocent term without today's narcotic connotation that described the individual who propelled the motorless chair at hair-raising speeds of four miles per hour. By the turn of the century there were hundreds of chairs on the Atlantic City Boardwalk, many of which were smartly varnished and equipped with flat Japanese umbrellas for protection from the sun.

The rolling chair romanticized Boardwalk transportation in Atlantic City in the early 1900s. Rolling chairs, after years of inactivity, are back in use in Atlantic City today. *Photo from the book* Atlantic City: 125 Years of Ocean Madness *by Vicki Gold Levi et al.*

The chairs, initially intended by Shill for handicapped persons, were favorites of board walkers of all shapes and sizes. A 1905 news report suggests that the mayor of Atlantic City became concerned about the safety of the chairs after he was nearly flattened by one and its 200-pound female occupant. As a result, the city council established a special 10-man force to police Sunday's "rush hour" rolling chair traffic and slap the wrists of careless pushers.

IMMORTALIZED IN SONG

The rolling chair inspired a popular song in 1905 called "Why Don't You Try?" It asks the question, "Did you ever see a maiden in a little rolling chair?" and is widely known merely as "The Rolling Chair Song."

ROLLING TO THE END OF AN ERA

The motorless rolling chair went the way of the horse and buggy after World War II, when electric chairmobiles made their debut on the Boardwalk. In 1948, Atlantic City passed an ordinance limiting the number of electric chairs on the Boardwalk to 100 and requiring that they maintain a maximum speed of just four miles per hour. And they were not permitted to carry bells, horns, or other noise-making devices.

Leisure and Lifestyle

SCHOOL FOR DOG GUIDES FOR BLIND PEOPLE

The Seeing Eye, Inc. is to dog guides what Kleenex is to the tissue business. In 1929, the Morristown, Morris County–based company opened North America's first dog guide school. And while the term "Seeing Eye" has since been used to describe dog guides in general, it is actually a registered trademark for canine graduates of The Seeing Eye.

This pioneer school was founded by a Philadelphia woman, Dorothy Harrison Eustis. While living in Switzerland, Eustis bred German shepherd dogs for desirable character traits such as alertness, stamina, and responsibility. She measured the breeding program's effectiveness by the dogs' ability to be trained to perform responsible tasks. Her canine graduates ultimately served admirably for the Swiss Army and several metropolitan police units in Europe.

But Eustis was not aware of the dogs' full potential until she visited a European school where German shepherds were being trained as guides for blinded veterans of World War I. She was so impressed that she wrote an article for the *Saturday Evening Post* (November 5, 1927) entitled "The Seeing Eye." This article reached a young man named Morris Frank in Tennessee and he wrote to Eustis: "...Thousands of blind like me abhor being dependent on others. Help me and I will help them. Train me and I will bring back my dog and show people here how a blind man can be absolutely on his own."

Frank was invited to Switzerland, where Eustis selected and trained a dog for him. Then he was trained with the dog. Frank and his dog,

Morris Frank, Dorothy Harrison Eustis, and guide dog Buddy, shown in 1936, were the pioneers of guide dog training. *Courtesy of The Seeing Eye, Morristown, New Jersey*

Buddy, returned to the United States and together they successfully confronted every conceivable traffic situation. It was this success that led Mrs. Eustis to return to the United States to establish The Seeing Eye.

Preparing for Their Final Exam

Puppies from The Seeing Eye program are placed with volunteer families at about age eight weeks. They are nurtured and taught basic obedience by these volunteers for about 16 months. The dogs are then placed with instructors at The Seeing Eye for a four-month training course. They are taught to respond to a system of rewards and corrections—the rewards often no more than a loving pat and the corrections no harsher than a verbal reprimand.

The dogs begin training on the quiet residential streets of Morristown, where they are taught to pull out and lead in harness and to stop at curbs. The training routes eventually become more congested with automotive and pedestrian traffic and the dogs are ultimately taught "intelligent dis-obedience"—the ability to disregard a command if it would lead to danger. At the conclusion of the four-month course, the dogs are ready for a "final exam." Instructors wear blindfolds and walk their dogs in Morristown while a training supervisor evaluates them. Only if it passes this final exam is a dog placed with a blind person. The blind person will spend an additional three to four weeks learning to live and work with the dog.

Inside the Numbers

Since its founding in 1929, The Seeing Eye has matched more than 11,000 dogs with blind men and women:

- It has placed dogs in all 50 states, the District of Columbia, Puerto Rico, and Canada.
- Its 1,800 active canine graduates work with students, teachers, lawyers, homemakers, clergy, masseurs, musicians, factory workers, piano tuners, writers, vending stand operators, and more.
- About 80 percent of the dogs used by The Seeing Eye are German shep-herds and Labrador retrievers.
- The Seeing Eye dogs generally work for about 8 to 10 years before retir-ing. After retirement, they may remain with their master as a pet or be placed with a new owner as a pet.

Money Is Not an Object

Blind or visually impaired people in their late teens or older, who are in good physical condition, may apply to The Seeing Eye. Each student is asked to assume an obligation of about $150 for his or her first visit and

$50 for each subsequent visit. This amount is applied to the cost of the dog and its initial training, instruction with the dog, room and board for the 20 to 27 days the student spends at the school, round-trip transportation from anywhere in the United States or Canada, and lifetime follow-up services. The payment covers just a fraction of the total cost. The difference is made up through philanthropic gifts. No one has ever been denied a Seeing Eye dog for lack of funds.

New Jersey was the first state to pass legislation guaranteeing equal access to all public places and accommodations for blind people accompanied by dog guides, according to The Seeing Eye. This legislation was the direct result of lobbying by Morris Frank and Buddy, the first Seeing Eye team.

☞ To Visit: The Seeing Eye Campus

The Seeing Eye's 60-acre campus has been at its present location since 1965 and features a 24-room student residence with exercise room, library/technology center, and dining room; the Walker Dillard Kirby Canine Center, which houses 120 dogs in training; and a state-of-the-art veterinary facility.

The Seeing Eye
P.O. Box 375
Morristown, NJ 07963-0375
973-539-4425, ext. 762
Free, two-hour public tours on selected Monday and Thursday mornings. Reservations are necessary.

AREA CODES AND THE DIRECT-DIAL LONG-DISTANCE CALL

When the mayor of Englewood, New Jersey, placed a phone call to the mayor of Alameda, California, on November 10, 1951, it marked two firsts for New Jersey.

The call *did not* require an operator's assistance, making the mayors' conversation the first direct-dial long-distance phone call. Previously, 10-digit direct dialing did not exist; any long-distance calls required the services of an operator. What that phone call *did* require was the use of area codes. New Jersey, without doubt benefiting from the favoritism shown by native son Bell Telephone, was assigned the first area code for that 1951 phone call—the granddaddy of all area codes, 201.

Much has changed in the world of area codes since the mayors talked. First, New Jersey underwent one of the earliest area code splits in the 1960s when southern New Jersey was assigned the 609 code. Ultimately, area code 201 was split again, to add the new 908 area code in 1991. Just six years later, 201 and 908 both split again (adding area codes 973 and 732) to give northern New Jersey four area codes. The state's total will increase to six when area code 609, untouched since its split with 201, will itself divide.

TWO WAYS TO CREATE A NEW AREA CODE

The most common method is to split an existing area code into two using geographic guidelines. Under this "division" technique, up to half of an area code's customers would see their area code change. Two businesses on opposite sides of the street (which were previously in the same area code) could now have different area codes.

A second method is called an "overlay," where only new numbers are assigned to the new area code. Existing numbers would not be subject to change, but under this situation an existing business or household that adds a phone line after the overlay would have two different area codes for lines in the same building or home.

Through all the years and all the splits and even the 1984 breakup of the Bell system, Englewood has weathered the storm. It remains firmly embedded in area code 201—now just a shadow of its former self in a small area in far northeast New Jersey. On the other end of the line, however, Alameda received that first direct-dial long-distance call in 1951 as part of area code 415, but it is now part of the split-created 510 area code.

Bellcore, the Morristown-based Bell system descendant that handles the assignment of area codes, has downplayed the significance of the changes, which generally wreak havoc on speed dialing for the technologically impaired and create writer's cramp for those who must send out new business cards to replace their repeatedly outdated ones. "We view them differently," Bellcore spokesman Ken Branson told the *New York Times*. "To us [area codes] are not cultural icons. They were not left here when the glaciers retreated. They are not mentioned in the Constitution. They are buckets with numbers in them."

Additional phone lines required for fax machines and on-line computer service—at work and at home—plus pagers and cell phones have helped fill those buckets, which hold about 7.9 million phone numbers each.

PLAYING FAVORITES?

Even Bellcore, the company that now handles the assignment and creation of area codes, has not been immune to the area code controversy. Bellcore's Morristown headquarters recently switched from 201 to 973, and its Piscataway office shifted from 908 to 732. Apparently, it's not who you know....

The critical, high-profile role that New Jersey played during the Revolutionary War and the formation of the United States is undisputed and well documented. It is also well maintained in the form of the country's first National Historic Park in Morristown, Morris County. The park was created in 1933 as the National Park Service's first *historic* park. The Morristown park, which covers 1,700 acres, is not the first national park—that distinction belongs to Yellowstone National Park (1872). Morristown N.H.P., however, is the first national park to recognize the need to preserve historic significance rather than natural resources.

It is estimated that more than 10,000 people were on the lawn of the Jacob Ford Mansion when the park was dedicated in 1933—the year when an executive order by President Roosevelt gave the National Park Service control of military parks, battlefield sites and cemeteries, and other memorials previously maintained by the Departments of War and Agriculture. Today, the National Park Service estimates that nearly 600,000 people visit the park each year.

Structures and History Are Preserved

The park preserves sites in Morristown occupied by General George Washington and some 10,000 soldiers of the Continental Army during the Revolutionary War from December 1779 to June 1780. According to the National Park Service, Washington chose the area for its logistical, geographical, and topographical military advantages and its proximity to New York City, which was occupied by the British in 1779.

The park is actually composed of four non-contiguous sections. Among the structures preserved is the Ford Mansion, which General Washington (accompanied by wife Martha) used as his headquarters during the winter of 1779-80. The Ford Mansion was built between 1772 and 1774 by Colonel Jacob Ford, who died of pneumonia in 1777 while serving in the

Continental Army. His widow willingly provided the home to Washington. It has been restored as an example of colonial affluence and also houses a museum and library.

Also preserved are the Upper Redoubt site, which was built in 1777 in the Fort Nonsense unit of the park following the battles of Princeton and Trenton; the historic Wick House and Farm, which served as the headquarters for General Arthur St. Clair; and the 18th-century Guerin House, which was restored in the 1930s and is used today as a private residence inaccessible to the public. New York City is visible from the Fort Nonsense unit of the park.

The Jockey Hollow unit of the park provides visitors with more than 27 miles of hiking and horse trails as well as five replicas of soldier huts (there were some 1,200 in 1779 on the site). Its visitor center offers a 10-minute film on civilian and military life in 1779.

☞ To Visit: Morristown National Historic Park

Morristown National Historic Park
Washington Place
Morristown, NJ 07960
973-539-2085
www.nps.gov
Hours: Daily, 9 A.M.-5 P.M.
Closed Thanksgiving, Christmas, and New Year's Day.
Admission charged; children under 17 are admitted free.

FM RADIO

Edwin Howard Armstrong's pioneering work in electrical engineering resulted in the invention of three of the basic electronic circuits underlying all modern radio, television, and radar, including frequency modulation, or FM radio.

Born in 1890, Armstrong was a junior at Columbia University in New York City in 1912, when he devised a regenerative circuit that produced not only the first radio amplifier, but also the key component of the continuous-wave transmitter that remains at the heart of all radio operations.

Armstrong was a member of the U.S. Army Signal Corps during World War I and was sent to Paris. His mission: to detect possible inaudible short-wave communications by enemies of the Allied Forces. Utilizing a technique called heterodyning, Armstrong produced an eight-tube receiver. In tests conducted from the Eiffel Tower, the receiver was able to amplify weak signals at levels not thought possible. Armstrong called this the heterodyne circuit. While it did not detect any enemy transmissions during the war, it is a common circuit used today by many radio and television receivers.

Skeptics Abound

By 1930, Armstrong turned his attention to a new problem: the elimination of radio static. His goal was to design a system in which the carrier-wave frequency would be modulated while the amplitude stayed constant. While Armstrong's theories were met with skepticism by some of his colleagues, he did discover a wide-based frequency modulation (FM) system in 1933. In field tests, the FM system provided clear reception during the most violent weather and also produced the highest-fidelity sound heard to date on the radio.

It took Armstrong seven years—until 1940—to receive a permit for the first FM station, which was erected along with a 425-foot tower on the Hudson River Palisades in Alpine, Bergen County. Then it took another two years before Armstrong was able to receive some frequency allocations from the Federal Communications Commission.

FM broadcasting began to grow after World War II and got a boost in the 1960s after the federal government ordered that all new radio sets and car radios offer FM. But Armstrong would not live long enough to see it become a national broadcasting power. The FCC placed FM on a frequency band at limited power while Armstrong faced legal challenges from a variety of corporations over the rights to his inventions.

In ill health, Armstrong committed suicide in 1954. His widow eventually would win a $10 million settlement in damages from infringement suits regarding his inventions. While Armstrong's name may not be remembered by the general public today, his influence can be heard every time someone tunes in to an FM station.

ON A LEVEL WITH BELL

Edwin Armstrong was made a charter member of the New Jersey Inventors Hall of Fame at the New Jersey Institute of Technology in March 1989. And the International Telecommunications Union in Geneva, Switzerland, has recognized his work and placed it on a level with that of such inventors as Alexander Graham Bell.

AIR CONDITIONING

Willis Haviland Carrier was just a year out of Cornell University when, in 1902, he crossed paths with a frustrated Brooklyn printer who was quite unhappy that changes in temperature and humidity at his business were hindering his ability to produce high-quality results.

Carrier solved that printer's problem. He designed and installed a spray-type system that helped cool air temperature and regulate humidity, allowing the disgruntled printer to avoid changes in paper dimensions and ink colors. Four years later, Carrier obtained his first patent on the product, "An Apparatus for Treating Air."

For nearly two decades, scientific air conditioning systems benefited machines and industrial processes (southern U.S. textile mills and even a silk mill in Yokohama, Japan, were early customers) but did little for the comfort of people. After all, people of the early 1900s had never experienced air conditioning; they had no idea what they were missing!

Air Conditioning Breakthrough

Riding a wave of industrial success, Carrier and six friends raised $32,600 to form the Carrier Engineering Company in Newark, Essex County, in 1915. Carrier Engineering began manufacturing products in 1922 after Willis Carrier developed the breakthrough centrifugal refrigeration machine, which provided the first safe and practical method of air conditioning large areas. It is believed that this single achievement paved the way for the upward expansion of cities, as well as bringing human comfort to hospitals, schools, office buildings, airports, and department stores.

The first "comfort" cooling took place at the J.L. Hudson department store in Detroit in 1924. Prior to the installation of three Carrier centrifugal chillers, customers battling the large crowds would faint at the store's popular basement sales. And it was Carrier's New Jersey–built air conditioning systems that revived summer business at theaters throughout the country in the 1920s. By 1930, 300 of them were air conditioned by Carrier systems.

A GAIN IN POPULARITY

The popularity of comfort air conditioning moved slowly from public places such as theaters and department stores to the home. By 1955, only 430,000 homes in the United States were equipped with central air conditioning, but by 1965, that number had grown to three million. And by 1975, 36 percent of all homes being built were air conditioned. Another 10 years later, 70 percent of new homes included air conditioning; that number rose to nearly 90 percent in Southern homes, making room for the dramatic growth of the Sunbelt.

GAY AND LESBIAN ADOPTION

Bergen County Superior Court Judge Sybil R. Moses approved a consent judgment on December 17, 1997, that allows for joint adoption of children by gay and lesbian couples, making New Jersey the first state in the country to provide such equal footing for gay families.

The consent judgment was negotiated by attorneys for the American Civil Liberties Union and state attorneys as the resolution of a class action lawsuit brought by the ACLU, the gay and lesbian family organization Lambda Families, and a gay male couple, Jon Holden and Michael Galluccio, from Maplewood, Essex County, who sought to jointly adopt their two-year-old foster son, Adam.

ACLU attorneys challenged a policy devised by the state's Department of Youth and Family Services (DYFS) to prohibit joint adoptions by unmarried partners. The ACLU claimed that policy violated equal protection guarantees and was inconsistent with state adoption law, which requires that a child's best interest take precedence. Judge Moses' approval of the parties' consent judgment—which is a written document entered in court describing the settlement of the dispute—effectively makes the agreement the law of the state.

With the agreement, New Jersey became the first state in the nation to specify that gay and unmarried couples will be judged by the same adoption standards as married couples, and that no couple will be barred from adopting because of their sexual orientation or marital status. (The judgment also applies to unmarried heterosexual couples living in New Jersey.)

Lenora M. Lapidus, legal director of the ACLU of New Jersey, called the agreement a "complete and total victory for gay families, equal rights and the thousands of children in the state waiting to be adopted." She said the settlement guarantees that all couples seeking adoptions will be judged "only by their ability to love and support a child."

FIRST CITY WITH INCANDESCENT STREET LIGHTING

No one said "Let there be light," but the town of Roselle, Union County, made history on January 19, 1883, when it became the first municipality in the United States to light its streets with incandescent bulbs. Four years after Thomas Edison lit the first incandescent lamp at Menlo Park, Essex County, Roselle proved the lighting system would work on a municipal-wide basis.

Since 1879, the Company for Isolated Lighting had set up more than 100 isolated plants, which provided lights for stores, hotels, newspapers, and other businesses, including the *Philadelphia Tribune* and the *New York Herald*. The next step was to provide lighting for a small town. Edison preferred that a town be chosen in the vicinity of New York City, and Roselle, with a population of 2,000, fit the bill.

A Bargain at a Buck a Year

Operations began in the fall of 1882, when the Edison Company received a franchise from the Roselle Land and Improvement Authority that lighting would be provided at a nominal cost of one dollar per year. The work included the installation of street lamps and the construction of a central power station for illumination.

As with any change, some people feared the coming of electricity, feeling more comfortable with gas lighting or candles. Edison was convinced of the invention's potential but realized he had to win the hearts and minds of the public for incandescent lighting to succeed on a mass basis. "My greatest trouble," he predicted, "will be to get the people to use the lights."

Delays in obtaining the equipment pushed back the projected start of the lighting from November to December, then to mid-January. Finally, on January 19, 1883, residents of the town gathered at the Mansion House Hotel for the much-anticipated debut. After a series of last-minute checks at the illuminating station, the lights went on in Roselle. The success of incandescent lighting in that small town would forever change the way Americans worked and played.

NEW MEANING TO "SEEING THE LIGHT"

The First Presbyterian Church at Fifth Avenue and Chestnut Street in Roselle would become the first American church to be lit with incandescent lighting.

STANDARD TIME

"Does anybody really know what time it is?" the rock group Chicago asked in its Top 10 hit of the same name in 1970. Thanks to the actions of William F. Allen of South Orange, Essex County, nearly a century earlier in 1883, the answer is "yes!"

Allen's plan was simple but carried a great impact: He introduced the first use of standard time in the United States. A railroad employee since 1862 and the son of a career railroad man from Bordentown, Burlington County, Allen had been perplexed by the confusing schedules used by railroads. Under the concept of "railroad time," all watches and other time-pieces were set by the position of the sun in the sky.

That meant, for example, that high noon in Boston would not correspond to the time in other major Eastern cities, such as New York or Philadelphia. In big city train stations, where a half dozen major railroads would converge, each rail line used the time of its office in its home city. Departing passengers were confused by the variety of times listed at the train station. And this was at a time when trains were the dominant form of transportation in the United States.

A Matter of Timing

Allen was chosen as a secretary of the General Time Convention in 1875. Its goal was to establish a uniform time policy for all the railroads from New York to California. It took eight years for the railroads to adopt Allen's plan of dividing the continental United States into four time zones that are known today as Eastern, Central, Mountain, and Pacific. The four zones each cover about 15 degrees of longitude. Railroad workers and their passengers would no longer be confused about what time trains would arrive and depart, for if it was 11 A.M. in Washington, D.C., it was also 11 A.M. in Boston, Cleveland, and every other town and city in the Eastern time zone.

The big change took place on November 18, 1883, when Allen's plan momentarily stopped all clocks at high noon so that they could be reset to the "standard" time. Allen's timely plan would help unify the country in an area that sorely needed uniformity and provide an economic lift to the business world.

WAR TIME CHANGES

Standard time allowed room for adjustments, particularly in periods of war. During World War I, daylight-saving time was adopted in various countries; clocks were set ahead one hour to save fuel by reducing the need for artificial lighting in evening hours. During World War II, all clocks in the United States were kept one hour ahead of standard time between February 9, 1942, and September 30, 1945. Daylight-saving time is now observed in most states from the first Sunday in April until the last Sunday in October.

SANTA CLAUS

Santa Claus may now reside at the North Pole, but he spent his formative years in New Jersey.

The Santa that children of all ages have come to know and love—the jolly, chubby man with a long white beard, black boots, and red suit—is the work of cartoonist Thomas Nast, who spent 30 years in Morristown, Morris County, creating St. Nick and other illustrated icons such as the Republican Elephant, the Democratic Donkey, and "Uncle Sam."

Widely recognized as the father of the American political cartoon, Nast was born in Germany in 1840; he came to the United States at age 6 and was drawing commercially to help support his family by the ripe old age of 15. When he was 22, he joined the staff of *Harper's Weekly*, one of the country's most prestigious magazines, and served as a war correspondent by producing on-the-scene sketches.

It was for *Harper's Weekly* that each Christmas, beginning in 1863, Nast drew holiday scenes featuring Santa Claus (his first illustration showed Santa distributing gifts to Union troops). While prior to this time there were many visual interpretations of how Santa appeared (from gnome-like figure to stern patriarch in bishop's robes), Nast based his drawings of

Santa Claus on the jolly figure described in Clement Moore's poem, "A Visit from St. Nicholas," which is perhaps better known as "The Night Before Christmas." Moore's vision of Santa included his wardrobe ("dressed all in fur, from his head to his foot"), his complexion ("his cheeks were like roses, his nose like a cherry"), his build ("a broad face and a little round belly...he was chubby and plump"), and even his demeanor ("he laughed like a bowlful of jelly").

Using Moore's description, Nast's vision of Santa Claus really sprang to life when many of the annual drawings from *Harper's Weekly* were compiled and published in a book, *Christmas Drawings for the Human Race*, that was sold during the Christmas season in 1890. The book also included new color paintings of Santa, and for the first time he could be seen in his red suit with white fur and big black belt. Nast developed Santa further over the years by adding his toy-making workshop to the cartoons and even incorporating a list of good children and bad children into his illustrations.

Nast moved from New York City to Morristown in 1872; many of his Santa Claus drawings originated from his home, Villa Fontana, which is now a National Historic Landmark. The Nast home was a common meet-

MORE THAN MERRIMENT

While Thomas Nast's drawings of Santa Claus had a wide impact, the Morristown cartoonist's real clout came in the political arena. Every presidential candidate supported by Nast in his drawings was elected. His cartoons exposed the corrupt "Boss" Tweed of Tammany Hall in New York City. He drew the character we recognize as Uncle Sam. And it was Nast who defined political parties by elephant (Republican) and donkey (Democrat) in a cartoon in *Harper's Weekly* in 1874.

ing ground for the artistic community in Morristown and hosted prominent visitors such as Ulysses S. Grant and Mark Twain. Thomas Nast's home at 50 Macculloch Avenue in Morristown is restored and now privately owned.

☞ To Visit: The Works of Thomas Nast

The Thomas Nast Society honors Nast each year and helps display a collection of his work at the Macculloch Hall Historical Museum. For more information, contact:

The Thomas Nast Society
c/o Morristown-Morris Township Public Library
1 Miller Road
Morristown, NJ 07960
973-538-3473

A Matter of Business

THE FIRST REPEATING FIREARM

Whoever first said "war is hell" was clearly not in the business of making guns. Samuel Colt founded the Patent Arms Manufacturing Business in Paterson, Passaic County, in 1836 to begin production of the first U.S.-made repeating firearm, the Colt revolver—the infamous "six-shooter" that helped spin so many stories of the wild, wild West.

Colt's automatic weapon had a spinning cylinder in it that automatically loaded the next bullet into position after each shot was fired. But Colt's business venture, launched in northern New Jersey when he was just 22 years old, was far from a runaway success. In fact, the manufacturing operation went bankrupt six years after it opened when Colt couldn't generate enough interest in the six-shooter.

Colt's revolver made a big comeback in 1846, however, when it became a beneficiary of the Mexican War. Texans fighting to remain independent from Mexico from 1846 to 1848 greatly appreciated the revolver's repeating action and helped restore its place in the history of American weaponry.

FIRST SUCCESSFUL GLASS COMPANY IN THE UNITED STATES

Glass has become such a commonplace component of everyday living that, like the air we breathe, it's often taken for granted. It's an essential element of our homes, workplaces, and modes of transport. It is used in kitchens and computers. It helped put a man on the moon and improved the eyesight of millions.

The first successful glass company in the United States has its origins in colonial New Jersey and predates the signing of the Declaration of Independence by more than 35 years. The Wistarburgh Glassworks began production in 1739 in Alloway, Salem County.

Family Affair

Built by Caspar Wistar, a successful businessman in Philadelphia (and grandfather of the well-known physician), and continued by his son, Richard, the company produced glass until 1777, two years after the beginning of the Revolutionary War. The Wistars played an important part in the development of the American glass industry by bringing glassmaking traditions from their native Germany through the craftsmen they hired.

Caspar Wistar acquired more than 2,000 acres of land along Alloways Creek in 1738 for his glassworks. The site, located eight miles from Salem, was ideally suited for glass production. The wooded area provided fuel for the glassmaking furnaces, while nearby Alloways Creek allowed for easy transportation of raw materials and finished product. The silica sand found in southern New Jersey was an excellent sand for making glass. The remoteness of the area offered another advantage for Wistar. He could hide his operation from the British, who prohibited the manufacturing of glass products in the colonies so that they would be compelled to buy glass from the mother country.

Production at the glassworks was centered around functional items that could be used in the home: window panes, bottles, jars, sugar bowls, cream jugs, and salt dishes. While Wistarburgh produced glass for less than 40 years, its importance cannot be underestimated. It laid the foundation for an industry that would flourish in the 19th and 20th centuries and that continues to be part of the New Jersey landscape today.

At one time, there were more than 200 glass factories in New Jersey, including one in Glassboro, Gloucester County, named for its formerly thriving glass industry. Today, there are 15.

FIRST GLASS BOTTLE TALLER THAN TALLEST NBA PLAYER

Glass-making is as much a part of New Jersey's heritage as the tomato, the shore, and the Pinelands. A team of glassblowers at the T.C. Wheaton Glass Factory at Wheaton Village in Millville, Cumberland County, demonstrated this when they produced the first bottle bigger than any National Basketball Association player. The 188-gallon bottle stands seven feet, eight inches tall, or about an inch taller than former Philadelphia 76er center Manute Bol. It has been recognized as the world's largest bottle by the *Guinness Book of World Records*.

Internationally renowned glass artist Steven Tobin and his team of Dale Leader, Daisuke Shintani, Don Friel, David Lewin, and Chuck Smart practiced for months to perfect the process they used to create the bottle. "We have had to build on the efforts of those glass artists who have come before us in developing the techniques necessary to blow a bottle of this size," Tobin recalled. "It has been an education for all of us."

"Glass Blast"

The record-setting event took place, fittingly enough, on September 26, 1992, during "Glass Blast" weekend, an event designed to celebrate the tradition of South Jersey glassmaking. Working at temperatures that reached 2,200°F—more than 10 times the temperature needed to boil water—Tobin placed a 54-inch stainless steel blowpipe into a furnace of molten glass and turned it around to form a small gather. A small bubble was blown into the gather. Over and over, the team returned to the furnace to gather more molten glass, which at very high temperatures drips like honey.

Layers of glass were piled on the original gather. "It resembled the layers of skin on an onion," Friel said. "We shaped it, let it cool and went back. Each time, the size of the gather was twice what it was before. When the blowpipe was taken out of the furnace for the sixth time, the gather weighed about 90 pounds."

Its weight felt closer to 200 pounds since it was at the end of the blowpipe, team members said. It took four members of the team to carry the blowpipe to a four-foot-tall, specially designed metal mold made from a steel drum lined with wooden slats. On a set of steps, Shintani attached a hose to the blowpipe's neck, which measured an inch and a half in diameter, and began inflating the gather with compressed air. As it stretched and grew, a team member raised the steps with a forklift. Using torches, Tobin and Lewin reheated the glass as Shintani kept lengthening the bottle with an air hose. When the bottle reached seven feet, eight inches, it was removed from the mold.

Fast Action

The workers had to act quickly since the bottle's thin walls cooled rapidly and could shatter easily. The bottle had to be shifted from its vertical position to its side so it could be placed in a specially built annealing oven. A fire-resistant fabric sling was used to transport the bottle. Four team members transferred the bottle to the oven and two team members opened the oven door in a matter of seconds to keep the bottle from breaking. Once in the oven, the blowpipe had to be broken off. This was done by scoring the bottle with a file and then hitting it with a baseball bat to separate the blowpipe.

Because of the thinness of the glass, the bottle was removed from the oven after 20 hours so it would not crack. The glass-blowing team had made history by creating a bottle that even Manute Bol could look up to.

The seven-foot, eight-inch bottle is on permanent exhibit today at the Museum of American Glass at Wheaton Village in Millville.

☞ *To Visit: Museum of American Glass*

The Museum of American Glass at Wheaton Village in Millville, Cumberland County, offers a look at New Jersey glass production with a wide variety of glass exhibits and a replica of a 19th-century glass factory. The world's largest bottle is on permanent exhibit there.

Museum of American Glass
Wheaton Village
1501 Glasstown Road
Millville, NJ 08332
609-825-6800
Hours: Daily, 10 A.M.-5 P.M.
Closed New Year's Day, Easter, Thanksgiving, and Christmas. The village is also closed on Mondays and Tuesdays in January, February, and March. Admission charged; children age 5 and under are admitted free.

PATENT LEATHER AND MALLEABLE IRON

His name is not as well known as Thomas Edison's, but the inventions of Seth Boyden of Newark, Essex County, helped lay the foundation for establishing the United States as an industrial power in its formative years.

Like Edison, Boyden demonstrated his versatility as an inventor in different periods of the 19th century. He produced the first patent leather in 1818 and the first malleable cast iron in the United States in 1826. Both inventions served as catalysts in the trend toward industrialization.

A native of New England, Boyden was 27 when he came to Newark in 1815 with his new wife and a device for cutting thick hide into thin slices. He came from a family of inventors. His father, also named Seth, had invented the leather-splitting machine that the younger Seth brought to Newark. His younger brother, Ukiah Atherton Boyden, designed a turbine water wheel for cotton mills at Lowell, Massachusetts. Ukiah Boyden's water wheel was adopted in many mills and power plants around the country because of its efficient use of energy.

Within three years of his arrival in Newark, Boyden had devised a new way of glazing leather through the application of several layers of varnish. He baked each application in the oven and polished the final application. Boyden dubbed the product "patent leather." However, in an ironic twist, Boyden did not seek a patent for his work. In his 1988 book, *Newark*, New

Jersey historian John T. Cunningham writes: "He [Boyden] felt that his discoveries should be public property, a philosophy that would keep him permanently poor as it enriched others. For Boyden, a problem solved was a solution discarded. He could not stick to anything merely for profit."

Big Boost for Business

Boyden's invention provided a big lift for the leather trade in Newark, for everything from saddles to shoes to clothing. He continued to look for new challenges for his inventive mind and focused his energies on making a malleable iron that could more easily be molded into shapes than could cast iron. Boyden accomplished this in July 1826 after a successful experiment in his kitchen furnace involving the refining and cooling of pig iron. While malleable iron existed in Europe, it was a closely guarded secret unavailable to industries in the United States until Boyden's discovery on a fitting day— July 4. Malleable iron provided a big boost for the iron business. In 1830, the East Jersey Iron Manufacturing Company built a plant in Boonton, Morris County, capable of producing two million pounds of malleable iron a year.

NO STOPPING HIM

Seth Boyden also developed a hat-forming machine and an inexpensive process for manufacturing sheet iron. He designed and built the first machines for manufacturing nails and cutting files, and he was credited with the development of the Hilton strawberry. Boyden was inducted as a charter member of the New Jersey Inventors Hall of Fame in 1989.

Boyden would continue to dabble in other areas. He built Newark's first steam engine in 1825 and built a locomotive strong enough to overcome steep grades near Newark in 1835. He participated in the California Gold Rush in 1849 but did not strike it rich. Boyden had lived a full life by the time of his death at age 82 on March 31, 1870. In tribute to him, Edison called Boyden "one of America's greatest inventors."

SUGGESTED READINGS

Cunningham, John T. *New Jersey: A Mirror on America*. Andover, N.J.: Afton, 1988.

Deford, Frank. *The Life and Times of Miss America*. New York: Viking, 1971.

DiClerico, James M., and Barry J. Pavelec. *The Jersey Game*. New Brunswick: Rutgers University Press, 1991.

Encyclopedia of New Jersey. New York: Somerset Publishers, 1994.

Gallagher, William B. *When Dinosaurs Roamed New Jersey*. New Brunswick: Rutgers University Press, 1997.

Haley, John W., and John von Hoelle. *Sound and Glory*. Wilmington, Del.: Dyne-American Publications, 1990.

Levi, Vicki Gold, et al. *Atlantic City: 125 Years of Ocean Madness*. 2d ed. Berkeley: Ten Speed Press, 1994.

McGoldrick, Neale, and Margaret Crocco. *Reclaiming Lost Ground: The Struggle for Woman Suffrage in New Jersey*. N.p., 1993.

Pierce, John R., and Arthur G. Tressler. *The Research State: A History of Science in New Jersey*. Princeton: D. Van Nostrand, 1964.

Reilly, H. V. Pat. *From the Balloon to the Moon: New Jersey's Amazing Aviation History*. Oradell, Pa.: H.V. Publishers, 1992.

Roberts, Russell. *Discover Hidden New Jersey*. New Brunswick: Rutgers University Press, 1995.

Salvini, Emil R. *Summer City by the Sea: Cape May, NJ—An Illustrated History*. Belleville, N.J.: Wheal-Grace Publications, 1995.

Wilson, Harold F. *The Story of the New Jersey Shore*. Princeton: D. Van Nostrand, 1964

Dear Reader,

If you enjoyed reading this book in Camino's Firsts series, you will want to purchase the titles listed below.
If you have suggestions for future titles in the series, let us know.

You can contact or order from us at:
Camino Books, Inc.
P.O. Box 59026
Philadelphia, PA 19102

All orders must be prepaid. Please add $5.95 for postage & handling for the first book, $1.00 for each additional book.

Pennsylvania Firsts
The Famous, Infamous, and Quirky of the Keystone State
Patrick M. Reynolds • 192 pages, 36 photographs, $9.95

Philly Firsts
The Famous, Infamous, and Quirky of the City of Brotherly Love
Janice L. Booker • 224 pages, 54 photographs, $9.95

California Firsts
The Famous, Infamous, and Quirky of the Golden State
Teri Davis Greenberg • 224 pages, 52 photographs, $9.95

Florida Firsts
The Famous, Infamous, and Quirky of the Sunshine State
Beverly Bryant Huttinger • 224 pages, 50 photographs, $9.95

Illinois Firsts
The Famous, Infamous, and Quirky of the Land of Lincoln
Lyndee Jobe Henderson • 224 pages, 48 photographs, $9.95

New Jersey Firsts
The Famous, Infamous, and Quirky of the Garden State
Harry Armstrong and Tom Wilk • 176 pages, 50 photographs, $9.95

www.caminobooks.com